HOW TO MEDITATE AND WHY

by Mara M. Zimmerman

BALBOA.
PRESS
A DIVISION OF HAY HOUSE

Balboa Press books may be ordered through booksellers or by contacting:

Balboa Press
A Division of Hay House
1663 Liberty Drive
Bloomington, IN 47403
www.balboapress.com
1 (877) 407-4847

Print information available on the last page.

ISBN: 978-1-5043-3346-7 (sc)
ISBN: 978-1-5043-3347-4 (hc)
ISBN: 978-1-5043-3348-1 (e)

Library of Congress Control Number: 2015908416

Balboa Press rev. date: 07/09/2015

For Tom, Willa and Effie

CONTENTS

ACKNOWLEDGEMENTS

I would like to thank my family, my parents, husband, children, and friends for their love and support and always encouraging me to reach my full potential and be true to myself. Special thanks to my editor, Alexia Paul, and to Hay House Publishing and Balboa Press for making this book possible. In addition, I would like to thank my teachers: my dear friend and mentor, Sonia Choquette, for her ongoing support and inspiration, and Paramhansa Yogananda, may his name be for a blessing, for his guidance. Finally, I would like to thank God, HaShem, for the love, guidance, and blessings I pray for and experience every day in my meditation and in my life.

FOREWORD

In my work as a spiritual teacher and consultant for over thirty-five years, I can say without reservation that there is no better practice – for mental, emotional, and physical well-being, as well as success in the world – than daily meditation. And yet, in spite of the overwhelming evidence of this truth, both in medical and mental health realms, few people embrace this wholesome, healing practice and make it their own.

In studying the individuals I have worked with, I have noticed three main reasons people resist meditation. The first is that few understand what meditation actually is, often believing it to be the practice of forcing themselves *not* to think, which is virtually impossible. Thus they become discouraged and frustrated, and quickly abandon their efforts altogether.

The second obstacle to this simple practice is people not fully understanding how meditation works. Outside of blindly taking the word of experts, they have little understanding of why such a simple practice can have such profound benefits to their overall well-being. In other words, it doesn't make sense, so they don't fully believe it is worth the effort.

And finally, meditation seems like such a huge, time-consuming, "you should do this," guilt tripping struggle that it doesn't take priority in people's lives. As a result, while some may want to meditate in theory, they don't actually put forward the effort needed to succeed because it brings with it burdens they don't want or need.

These obstacles need to be removed in order for someone unfamiliar with meditation to commit to this undertaking with any genuine enthusiasm – and stick with it. And that is why I adore Mara M. Zimmerman's book, *How to Meditate and Why*.

As my personal yoga instructor and long-time friend, I have experienced in Mara the gentle ability to address all of these obstacles with simplicity, clarity, and grace unlike any other teacher of meditation I have encountered. Mara dispels the myth that you have to follow a monk in order to meditate. Of course you can do this if you want to, but the truth is, as she shares in the book, people of all spiritual persuasions and backgrounds have meditated in their own way since the beginning of time. Mara lifts the veils of confusion that cloud meditation, and makes it accessible to everyone, no matter what their religious or spiritual background may be.

How to Meditate and Why lays out, in very simple terms, what actually occurs in the body when meditating, so it makes sense to those who need more evidence that meditation is useful to one's well-being from a practical standpoint, before they commit to trying it.

In demystifying meditation, Mara makes it inviting, gently guiding the reader into a meaningful experience, one simple and grounded breath at a time. Her book opens the way for all people to learn to successfully meditate even while managing the whirlwind of daily responsibilities that demand their time and attention.

She makes it so easy no one can fail.

Even though I am a seasoned practitioner of meditation, I still find Mara's gentle guidance to be of profound benefit to me, every day. With her help I know you, too, will soon look forward to meditation as the most important, grounding, and refreshing indulgence of your day. Enjoy.

Sonia Choquette
Author of the *New York Times* bestseller *The Answer is Simple*

INTRODUCTION

My journey

I tend to have a positive outlook on life. I see the potential in others and am very patient, sometimes too patient. But even my sunny nature gets a shadow sometimes, and I must check in to where I may have stepped out of alignment, allowed my integrity to be compromised, or just flat wore myself out. I meditate. I always have – long before I began to study, research, or seek a teacher. I needed to. I realized later that with my strong physical nature, I generally move at a very fast pace so I enjoy and benefit from slowing down. I also learned I have an introverted side to my extroverted self that I knew intuitively how to honor from an early age. Since I did not call it anything and never questioned it, I never stopped. In fact, it just kept growing as I did.

Allowing myself quiet time, without rhyme or reason, is the gift that keeps on giving. I was raised in a Jewish home in New York where I learned that blessings lit candles, and was shown the value of religious study, prayer, and Torah, which provided me a beautiful right of passage, opening my eyes to who I am and how diverse the world is. My parents encouraged me to be well educated. My mother taught me as a woman to have a strong voice, and my father showed me when and how to use it. My father was actually my first teacher of the gifts of quiet. I have looked to him all my life for sound advice and still do. As a great listener, he knows when to speak up and when to take pause and embrace the power of quiet.

As I grew, I searched for meaning and yearned to connect to the highest aspects of myself: my mind, body, and spirit. As a child, I was drawn to the aspects of sport that involved and encouraged visualization and a positive mental state of mind, allowing for less stimulation and more focus and insight. I later received a degree in Rehabilitation Counseling and Psychology and realized some people did not care for their bodies or their minds very well, if at all. The free spirit in me continued to search for more meaning, more blessings and more prayer, which I discovered through my beautiful family, weekly Shabbat, and daily yoga. I am blessed with a loving husband and our two incredible children. Our children are my teachers, and I seek meditation to help find answers to being a better parent and how to best care for them. Shabbat is a weekly Jewish tradition, which fulfills my need for ritual, connecting to my roots, each other, and to what is most important in my life. It acknowledges the value of taking time for the spirit, family, festive meals, standing, and sitting in prayer and meditation, community, rest and quiet.

Through yoga, I honor my physical body, its connection to my mind and spirit, and how I see myself and move in the world. As I focus on my breath, it takes my mind off other things. All the while I stretch, strengthen, and balance my body from movement into stillness, contemplation, and ultimately, meditation. Over time, I have continued to immerse myself in a natural lifestyle and pursued studies in Eastern philosophy and many Eastern healing techniques, yoga, meditation, and homeopathy. I have explored the wide variety of practices and benefits that meditation has to offer. This has ranged from absolute quiet by myself at home to classes locally and in India, to prayer and silence in a congregation and prayer at the Western Wall in Jerusalem.

My awareness, consciousness, creativity, and compassion have all grown and continue to grow with meditation as my guide. I have learned that the questions for me were not always *What will I do?* and *Am I good enough?* but *How will I do it?* and *Who will I be?*

Teaching meditation over the years has taught me many things. People are people wherever you go. Humans share certain qualities and traits, which make us similar in so many ways, yet we each possess individual personalities, wants and needs. Honoring our similarities and differences begins with knowing yourself and who you are. Choosing to be an active participant in your well-being for the greater good is a simple act of kindness you can give to yourself and others. The better we care for ourselves and find a balance of our wants and needs, the better we are in the world.

Your journey

Each of us is drawn to meditation for different reasons, perhaps to address a health problem, to relieve stress, recharge, change a lifestyle, for longevity, or even as a last resort. Some are drawn for physical reasons, others for emotional health or spiritual growth and awareness. Yet, the more you experience meditation, the more you uncover its gifts, including that of prevention. Of course, we cannot prevent everything, but we can prevent some things. We can also choose how we respond to things, especially if we are in touch with our feelings, our symptoms, and our senses. By paying attention and listening to the signs all around, you can notice more and miss less. By focusing and exercising your mind and gaining better concentration and awareness, you become more in tune and therefore more able to prevent things from escalating by better using your voice of reason. Meditation is not a one-size fits all practice, and there are as many ways to approach and embrace it, as there are reasons for seeking it. Whatever your reason, honor it.

Human life has always been challenging, full of the hardships that come with making a living, raising a family, caring for a household, and finding meaning and purpose. Most of us will encounter hardship and suffering, and many cope with physical, emotional, and mental conditions. Most people want the same things: quality of life with physical and mental health, love and companionship, understanding and wisdom, peace and freedom. Caring for our basic human needs sometimes falls apart at the seams and we are pulled in different directions, possibly getting sick or not having coping mechanisms to deal with daily life stress.

Getting in touch with yourself, paying closer attention, and embracing quiet can help you get re-centered, reconnected, more clear and bring you back to your whole self. Caring for your own needs allows you to better respond to the needs of others. Experiencing a sense of wholeness both in yourself and with the world around you – family, friends, pets, co-workers, your community small and large, the environment and all living things – helps you become integrated and connected. This is the foundation for wholeness and wellness in yourself and in your life.

Our Journey

Along with the effort of living, we must find time for peace, quiet, and rest with the intention to heal and become more balanced. Getting in touch with the bigger picture, and our individual selves even for a moment can bring many benefits and rewards. With all of the holidays, celebrations, and small and large successes along the way, there is enough good to go around and enough bad to move us into action. Let's be well enough to do so.

Meditation is a universal practice, with studies proving its many benefits. It need not be connected to any tradition, religion, or belief system. Access lies in the Self for greater awareness, discovery and self-reflection. Discover what it means to not just be human but a healthy, well functioning, and fundamentally good human with abilities, talents, and gifts to be harnessed and shared with love and compassion.

Your quality of life depends on your health and well-being. The best way is to begin at the beginning. Whether you are young or old, or somewhere in between, meditation provides a healing that is free of charge and accessible at any time.

This book offers stories, advice, history, method, and a philosophical guideline at a level approachable to all. There are many ways to approach meditation. Find yours and enjoy the benefits. Always remember, in meditation and in life, be happy from the smallest improvement.

PART I

A BACKGROUND ON MEDITATION

CHAPTER 1

WHAT IS MEDITATION?

"Meditation is active calmness." -*Paramhansa Yogananda*

The term meditation refers to a vast array of practices that include techniques designed to create awareness, promote inner peace, encourage well-being, as well as develop mindfulness, intuition, compassion and patience. Meditation supports efforts to regulate breathing and clear the mind, which can assist in stress relief, and may even ease many health issues.

Meditation is not a religion or lifestyle. It simply allows for a heightened awareness. This can range from awareness of your connection to the world to self-awareness. Becoming more self-aware allows you to have a clear perception and better understanding of who you are. Self-awareness allows for introspection and increased consciousness.

Meditation often evokes an image of someone sitting in a cross-legged position, eyes closed and burning incense, a religious person deep in prayer, or even an elite athlete in preparation. There are actually many different types and techniques of meditation. Remember, meditation is not necessarily one size fits all. Each person is unique and should be true to his or her own needs.

All forms of meditation involve harnessing the dynamics of the mind in order to think in a more intentional and less random or accidental manner. This can also help develop your intuition.

Most approaches to meditation entail a certain quieting of the mind and a sense of surrender to a higher or deeper aspect of the mind and of yourself. Whether your goal is metaphysical, to discover your true self, find purpose and meaning, achieve inner peace, heal, grieve, celebrate blessings, or even just take a moment to enjoy a little quiet, harmonizing your body and mind has the potential for many benefits. Meditation can promote physical, mental, and emotional wellness, assist in self-regulation, improve concentration, promote creative thinking, reduce the "monkey mind," promote relaxation and restoration, and enhance spiritual development.

Focusing on your breath is instant access to the beginning stages of meditation and connecting with yourself. Imagine someone suggested meditation to you for your high blood pressure. How would this work? Meditation is the science of the soul and spirit. Still, calming your mind and slowing your breath has an effect on your nervous and circulatory systems. After all, your brain and body are connected and must send clear signals to each other in order to read symptoms and register your immediate needs. For example, *I'm thirsty. I need water.* Or, *I'm tense. I need a break.* Honoring this direct connection, and taking good care of your body and mind, will ultimately lift your spirits.

Meditation is a training of the mind different from study and education. When the mind is stilled and there is quiet and pause, movement toward the best course of action is more accessible. So often we rush when only a moment would have created the opportunity to make a better decision. Meditation holds a key for self-control and behavior management, better problem solving, harnessing mindfulness, and possibly bringing treasures. The question is, will you notice them?

While there are many common misconceptions about meditation, what is important to know is that meditation is a goal and that *the process is relevant*. The spirit in which you do something is almost as important as the act itself. There are many activities that are key to the process in that they first restrict the mind so that you may begin meditation, which aims to expand it. Quieting the mind requires many steps in order to actually do so. These steps, many of which are discussed in Part III of this book, give purpose to the process and make the goal reachable. When you stop talking and get quiet, you can hear your breath and tune into yourself, which is difficult to do when there is too much noise.

A goal of meditation is to become interconnected and relieve stress – physically, mentally, and emotionally. This will allow for your spirit and energy to flow and grow. When we discuss focusing and restricting the mind in order to expand it, this is a new idea that may not be grasped right away. But the process in which to do so can be grasped immediately if only we can learn to be less attached to the outcome and more willing in the process.

Mind expansion occurs when we have realization, something beyond what we already know, beyond our current thoughts, beyond our immediate needs and wants, beyond our control. By focusing in on our breath, being still, being quiet and in the moment, we give our thoughts a chance to evolve. There is a relief after holding on so tightly and being so attached to everyone and everything, forgetting to think and overthink. Let go. Realize your gifts and abilities. Allow your true self to shine through.

Allow small stuff to be as important as the big stuff. Allow the moments in life that are most difficult to be your catalyst for meditative moments, taking a moment to be okay. Allow the easiest moments to also be an opportunity. Becoming more self-aware can assist you in becoming more sensitive and less self-absorbed. Tell someone you love them and give them a moment when you thought you had no time. Slow down at a yellow light instead of rushing through it. Become more discerning. Know better when to speak up and also when to embrace the wisdom of silence. Notice when you think it is all about you yet you are having a large effect on someone else. Notice if you are consistently trying to please others or gain their approval. Notice if you are expecting others to please you. We simply need to meet life where we are. Movement toward your goals takes time and care. Your effort, attitude and awareness are steps in the process of meditation – not just trying to get somewhere, but also realizing more and more the manner in which you approach your life.

Time passes no matter how you use it. Your mind thinks no matter what your thoughts are. Your breath and heart give you life whether you notice or not. People will need you no matter how you show up. Beginning to focus on the present and how you show up in life, at the best and the worst of times, has an effect greater than you may think. Restricting the mind to the present and learning to gain some control of your thoughts allows for a mind expansion you cannot bargain for. Whether you have a focus or intention when you begin or if you are simply sweeping the floor, training your mind to remain present is gained by discipline, practice, development, and patience. Quieting the mind can eventually lead you toward increased awareness of the bigger picture, ah-ha moments that you missed before. This awareness can shed light on circumstances that have not changed but you realized you can change in the way that you experience them.

When you prepare for a marathon you do not go out and run the full amount of miles the first time. You build up to the goal by beginning with a smaller goal.

Also, not everyone has the same reason for running. Some are interested in the mileage, some need the exercise or weight loss, others may be running for a cause or donation, yet others may simply enjoy running and have no other motivation. Meditation is like any other process in that you begin with where you are and expand from there. You try a few running sneakers on before you find the right ones. As you consider a few meditation techniques you may find a fit right away or may need to try out a few.

Even a moment of forgetting what you were thinking or trying to say is worth noting. When you "lose a thought" where does the thought go? Why is it we "lose" a thought when we are not trying to and have such difficulty forgetting a thought when we are trying to? How and why does it come back? We so often hold on to thoughts, which can be unhealthy if they are negative or not useful. We often will say to forget about it for a moment and suddenly, without notice, the thought returns. This happens in meditation when you are sitting still and quiet. The thoughts are there and then you "lose" them. Without warning, rhyme or reason. It simply happens. Allowing for the letting go of thought on purpose rather than "losing" them is a skill that develops over time. Read on to discover a variety of steps and techniques to assist in the process.

CHAPTER 2

A BRIEF HISTORY OF MEDITATION

*"This they call the highest state. When the 5 senses and the
mind are still, when not even reason stirs." -Upanishads*

Meditation is ancient. In one form or another, it has been practiced
by many of the great spiritual and religious practices worldwide.
Within these traditions one will find meditation in many different
forms.

When meditation is linked to a specific religion or culture, there
will naturally be differences of opinion and factual disputes. I am
writing to send the message that meditation need not be associated
with any of them. At the same time, age-old practices of all kinds
have many things to teach us. We can learn to act upon and apply
anything learned in a way that is suitable for our own interests,
needs, beliefs, and values. Many of us live in a time and place
of much independence and freedom. We are allowed to express
ourselves in all types of ways. How do we use our freedom? How
do we use our free time? People around the world have meditated
for many different reasons. What is your reason?

Your background and upbringing may be present in your
meditation experience but it also does not need to be. For those

who have less interest in spiritual aspects need not approach meditation from that point of view. If you have a body, breath, and a mind, the gifts of meditation are there for you with or without any connection to God, religion, or spiritual tradition. Having said that, the variety of meditation techniques that have existed over centuries offers many insights, ideas, and formulas for understanding meditation. I will touch upon some of the major faiths that contain a tradition of meditation.

Hinduism

From India comes the birth of yoga. In this tradition, meditation requires a process as described by the ancient yogis, and yoga serves as a good guideline. The Vedas are the original scriptures of Hindu teachings and the earliest literary record of Indian civilization. Veda means wisdom or knowledge. The Upanishads, or Vedanta, are inner or mystic teachings occurring in certain parts of the Vedas as essential summaries. They are the philosophical portion of the Vedas and are some of the oldest scriptures in the world to describe the practice of meditation.

Yoga can exist alongside the Hindu religion and its philosophical teachings are said to be universal. Yoga has always taught that meditation, the goal of yoga, is for all humankind. While the traditions and spirit of the Hindu culture are reachable, they can be separate from the teachings of meditation. The Hindu people brought their influence just as you can bring yours. Yoga has touched many traditions and people around the world. They may differ from one another in style, but in any case, meditation still remains the goal.

Prana is the Sanskrit word for energy, personal and universal, and the breath is the vehicle in which you carry your energy throughout your body. The ancient Rishi or Sage, Patanjali, was known to describe yoga as control of the fluctuations of the mind and as a means for becoming whole. His teachings in the Yoga Sutras of the eight limbs, eight petals or eightfold of yoga, are a wonderful and tangible guideline toward the goal of meditation as well as for well-being and quality of life.

Kirtan music is a call and response chanting accompanied by instruments, which creates a vibration in the body, having an effect on your mind and spirit. While it originates from Indian culture, it is said to be universal. Often sung in Sanskrit but heard in the West also in English, it aims to create a joyful mood and a path toward meditation.

Sikhism

Founded in India, Sikhs meditate to cope with life's everyday problems as well as to form a connection to the divine. Family life and spiritual life are interconnected and are rooted in Oneness and love. *Amritvela,* or early morning meditation, is a vital part of daily worship and life. This meditation occurs prior to dawn. This is considered to be the most opportune time for meditation, which is viewed as a doorway to consciousness. Yoga poses may be used to assist in clearing the mind for meditation. Kirtan music may also be practiced by Sikhs as a means for joy, enlightenment, and preparation for meditation.

Buddhism

In the story of Siddhartha, the boy who is later known as Gautama and eventually as Buddha was born a Hindu prince. He was hidden from witnessing any suffering in the world while confined to his palace as a boy. As time went on and the reality of the larger life outside the palace unfolded, he learned that the world contained great suffering, and he longed to see and know more. As he traveled, he tried different types of meditation, separating himself from society, fasting, and practicing acts of non-attachment. He soon learned that one cannot escape the world by fasting and meditating, nor is suffering avoidable. So he began a new path of moderation and middle ground, learning to be a seeker among the common people, gaining followers, including women, and guiding many to a life in which one is not sleeping but "awake" – the meaning of the word, Buddha.

Buddha eventually took his ideas on meditation further east, teaching it as a universal remedy for all ills. *Anapanasati*, used in Sanskrit and Chinese, means mindfulness of breathing, taught by the Buddha, to feel sensations caused by the movements of the breath in the body. One of his principal teachings was cessation of suffering and self-awakening. He taught that mindfulness is important and key in meditation.

Buddha taught basic technique on meditation by simply watching the breath. This suggested that anyone could meditate and tune into his or her energy through the breath. Buddha made clear in his teachings that focus on breathing alone can bring better concentration, helping to focus and live a meaningful, awakened life.

Judaism

Meditation in Judaism is ancient. The Hebrew word, *kavanah*, which means intention or more literally pointing the mind, is an essential part of Jewish life. *Shalom* implies not only peace, but also contemplation, completion and wholeness. *Tzedakah*, doing the "right" thing such as acts of charity, is highly valued and encourages compassion. These are all aspects of meditation.

Meditation and prayer in Judaism allow for pause. Jews honor and embrace ways to remember and continue on, to celebrate and show up for others, gaining self-knowledge by remembering the past and doing better in the future. Meditation and prayer are a part of daily life for good reason, keeping order from Shabbat to Shabbat and taking time to find peace and quiet.

Jews are offered a guideline and given a reason to be mindful, take pause and look within through Torah, the Old Testament. The Talmud is a rabbinic text containing the collection of teachings of Jewish law and tradition. Talmudic sages have a long-standing tradition of meditation before and during prayer. The Hebrew word for prayer, *tefillah*, implies connecting to and bonding with one's spirit source. Reading, reciting and chanting prayers and blessings allows for contemplation and their meaning to permeate one's consciousness.

When meditation is used as a remedy for stress and anxiety, it replaces negative emotions with the feeling of peace. Chassidic philosophy demonstrates how inner turmoil is reduced when we have a clear understanding of our goals, and how the cultivation of trust, faith, awareness, and freedom from doubt, enrich our lives with joy.

Judaism has ancient wisdom and teachings known as Kabbalah. Among Kabbalistic teachings is The Zohar, a book of spiritual and mystical teachings of Kabbalah. Traditionally, it was taught only to those who had reached the age of 40 and had already learned Torah and Talmud. In modern times, Kabbalah is taught more universally. Kabbalah demonstrates the need for introspection and asking questions regarding the Self and beyond. It is considered a source of personal and universal power and energy to heal and transform one's life and the world for the better. These are all aspects and goals of meditation.

Sufism

Sufism is an ancient mystical practice. Over time, it has evolved to people from different cultural backgrounds as a way of better understanding the truth of the universe and self-discovery. There is a letting go of dualistic attitudes and ideas. There is an inward focus and exploration with the Self, one's heart, energy and the soul. Meditation brings contemplation, meaning, and reflection or to think on a subject deeply, important aspects as we have seen in many meditation techniques. The famed mystic Rumi said, *"Yesterday I was clever, so I wanted to change the world. Today I am wise, so I am changing myself"*.

Taoism

Taoism was formed in ancient China and is a philosophical, ethical, and religious tradition that emphasizes living in harmony with the Tao or the "way," the universal life force that flows through and around all things. It is deeply rooted in Chinese customs and worldview. Taoist ideas have become popular throughout the world through different forms of martial arts. It teaches to embrace the wonder and joy in living gracefully and connecting with the natural world. Yin-Yang is perhaps the best known concept used within Taoism. Yin-Yang represent two complementary halves or forces that together complete wholeness. For example, night (Yin) and day (Yang).

Taoism teaches you to look within yourself. Taoist meditation is used to look inside one's self and discover his or her true nature.

Questions may be asked such as: *Who am I ? What is my purpose? How can I be of greatest service?* These reflect aspects of meditation taught in many great spiritual traditions.

Meditation is a means for discovering for yourself the answers to these deep questions through your own direct inner experience. Taoist meditation has less of an aim or a goal then you will see in other forms. The idea is to simply learn to "be" and not seek a specific outcome. The two primary guidelines are Jing (quiet, stillness, calm), and Ding (concentration and focus). The purpose of stillness is to turn your attention inward. Then one can concentrate and focus attention, usually on the breath, to develop what is known as 'single point awareness,' an undistracted state of mind, which permits intuitive insights to arise spontaneously.

Christianity

In Christianity, meditation is in the form of prayer. It is a reflection on religious study or practice. Its emphasis is oriented on reflective thinking on biblical scripture. Focus on prayer and guided meditation is a means for living a more meaningful life and can address stress and anxiety. Reflection on prayer and charity allow for and encourage compassion – an important aspect of meditation. Through New Age ideas and throughout time, some Christians have sought study and reflection of the Self. Kabbalah was popular among some Christian intellectuals during the Renaissance and Enlightenment periods. They adapted it for their own use. It is even reflected in the Tarot cards, which aimed to teach aspects of and connect with the Higher Self.

The Nobel Peace Prize winner Mother Teresa, who spent most of her life in India helping the poorest of the poor, was honored for her great compassion. She stated, *"We shall never know all the good a simple smile can do."*

Native American

Native American meditation and spirituality are based on the connection between humanity and the natural world, tapping into the spirit world, finding your spirit animal guides and connecting to nature. Drums and flutes are often used as a means for meditation. Ceremonial dancing and meditation relate to drumming like the heartbeat. Mother Earth and spirituality are a way of life and reflect the indigenous area in which they lived. With organized spiritual ceremonies and traditions, the earth is mother, the sky is father, and all things are interconnected. Meditation techniques are often combined with prayer to invoke the help of the Great Spirit and Ancestors.

Meditation can also be taking a walk in nature, experiencing interconnectedness with nature and life, or burning sage as a blessing and cleansing the environment and the human aura or energy body. This could also be a means to invite creativity or even improve harvest.

* * *

How you live your life, the choices you make, and actions you take are all aspects of meditation. You do not need to let go of your values and traditions in order to meditate. You can bring new ideas for growth to your current practice, ideas, values, and traditions. Remember, meditation has a history and you have yours. Meditation looks different wherever you go but can help you wherever you are.

CHAPTER 3

WHY MEDITATE?

"Peace comes from within." -Buddha

New Age has been kind to meditation, opening doors for the idea of self-realization and the power of the mind. All religions welcome, no religion necessary. Bring your spirit or leave it at home, offering philosophies from the East and scientific studies from the West. Meditation has much credibility and has shown a wide range of benefits for both the holy and the person with the holey jeans. Moments of silence for beauty and for tragedy connect diverse communities. The media spreads news around the world that inform us that we are not the only ones suffering and reminds us that we need to look within and also in the larger world around us.

There are many well-known figures that have helped increase the popularity of meditation and have learned or approached meditation for their own purpose and reasons. On her TV show on OWN, Oprah Winfrey found herself exploring meditation for the purpose of being still. She beautifully expressed the benefits of stillness, for example, creative expression and peace. Sting was in *The Telegraph* speaking about how yoga introduced him to a different style and approach to meditation. Expressing that the only meditation he would have done before would be in the writing of songs. Ellen DeGeneres has expressed positive results of her Transcendental Meditation experience, how it brings her peaceful feelings, and that she just cannot say enough good things about it.

Meditation is for common sense, pause, and remembering what matters most. Breathing and relaxing and knowing that your body rests while sleeping and your mind just might need some rest too.

So then if the spiritual and or religious seeker is given a guideline for meditation in one form or another in history or through current cultural luminaries, than what's in it for the average Joe? If so many ancient traditions have spiritual journeys, the question still begs, do I too have to be spiritual or religious in order to meditate? Must I pray and believe in something more? You do not have to carry any need for spiritual growth and development, but you can acknowledge those aspects are there. Meditating for the sake of meditating and nothing else is a wonderful way to be mindful. Not knowing why you need or want to meditate is just as good a start as any. Bring your own beliefs, values, wants and needs and know you are safe. Bring your judgment too – pack it in a bag, but please do leave your bag at the door. You can pick it up later. That is, if you still want to.

When I sit in meditation, I often begin with the intention of letting go of my thoughts and the feelings attached to them. Yet that may not happen immediately. I may also think of a problem that needs solving and begin by being quiet and letting go of the problem, focusing on my breath and sitting still or taking a walk. Problems often work themselves out if I back off and stop trying so hard, giving the issue at hand some time and space. Attacking every issue is not always useful. Patience is useful and giving a problem room to breathe can allow for intuition, insight, and clarity to enter the equation. We cannot always fix a problem immediately nor are we always in control. Plant seeds for a solution. Backing off may allow us to see a possibility or answer previously unseen.

There are many distractions in daily life, ranging from our physical selves, our emotional selves, our mental selves, our Higher Selves and the people with whom we interact with for better or for worse. Meditation is not just about sitting in quiet concentration but about *being* in quiet concentration.

The range of techniques that enhance the powers of the mind is used not only when actively meditating but also during daily life and sleep. Meditation touches upon most aspects of human experience and leads us to wisdom and awareness.

Know as you begin the process that you are a responsible person in a world of much responsibility. Management of time, emotional health, stress relief, and having enough energy to make it through the week are all rewards of meditation. Other benefits include:

- Getting more organized
- Goal setting
- Checking in on your self-care rituals such as good hygiene, good manners, and good habits
- Increased emotional health
- Behavior management
- Improved self-image
- Increased ability to be more present
- Mindfulness
- Increased focus and concentration
- Stress relief, relaxation and restoration
- Inner peace, calm and healing
- Pain management

- Improved sleep
- Intuition, insight and creativity
- Increased vitality
- Increased breathe awareness
- Gratitude for what you have and what is working for you
- Taking pause and noticing what is not working for you
- Helping others in ways that you can
- Reaching your full potential
- Forgiveness and Acceptance
- Self-love and compassion for yourself and others
- Grounding
- Spiritual growth

Practicing meditation is a way of living more intuitively. What feels right is right; what needs attention receives it. By adjusting and balancing within and around ourselves, we are able to direct our lives toward our goals and aspirations. We live a technology-filled, fast paced life, yet it must balance with other aspects of life that are not temporary and always exist.

Releasing emotional, mental, and physical blocks assists in bringing balance and homeostasis to your body, mind, and if you aspire to, your spirit. Recognizing your inner voice and having healthy actions to match and reflect it will help you reach your full potential and create a life that matters.

Though we cannot eliminate stress from our lives, meditation can help us manage it. Be mindful and tune into your degree of stress and your stress levels. Notice when your cup is overflowing and learn to relieve stress before becoming overwhelmed. Connect yourself to your own needs, your heart, purpose, and potential. Use your meditation practice to relax, restore, find wholeness, relieve stress, increase your focus, improve your concentration and develop better boundaries.

In this day and age, with access to the world's knowledge at our fingertips, it is easy to implement ancient forms of healing and blend and complement them with the miracles of modern medicine. Meditation is universal and may be useful in any lifestyle as well as any approach to your health. It can be used in the case of illness or disease in tandem with medications and surgery. It can aid in dealing with side effects of medication or recovery from addiction. It may replace negative thoughts and feelings with more positive ones bringing more inner calm and peace and helping in the healing process from grief and loss. It can help address weight issues and body image. Meditation can even support childbirth and child rearing.

The process of meditation continues to address your body even when you are at rest. Your cells have a memory and receive the oxygen circulation from both exercises of the body through physical movement but also through movement of the breath. The breath travels through your body and stores and restores. Oxygen gives us energy through our breath and the energy we have is connected to the quality of our breath. This is why physical exercise works well in helping to begin to balance your health. When we get the body moving, we are forced to get our breath moving. This gives the body more energy and vitality and gets the blood flowing so that unwanted toxins can move and exit the body and our minds, clearing the way for renewal.

Meditation is available to any and all from all walks of life. It is simple and accessible and you need not hold a belief system to meditate. There is no danger or threat. Relaxation and restoration are only a breath away. Learn to be great where you are. If you are interested in meditation for any reason, body, mind or spirit, read on to learn techniques to help you along the way.

PART II

UNDERSTANDING YOUR WHOLE SELF

CHAPTER 4

ACCESSING YOUR INTUITION

*"Have the courage to follow your heart
and intuition."* -Steve Jobs

Intuition

Intuition is defined as a direct perception of the truth, independent of any reasoning process – a quick, keen insight. It is an instant perception without conscious attention or reasoning, knowledge from within.

Helen Keller demonstrated that by illuminating the use of her sixth sense, her intuition, wonderful things could be accomplished. As she famously said, *"What I am looking for is not out there, it is in me"*.

Carl Jung also emphasized the importance of intuition. According to Jung, intuition is one of the four major functions of the human mind, along with sensation, thinking, and feeling. By balancing all of the functions within ourselves, we have the ability to maximize our potential. He regarded intuition as a basic psychological function that mediates perception in an unconscious way and enables us to experience the divine possibilities of a situation.

Developing your intuition is like learning any new skill. The more you practice, the better you get at it. That is, if you are practicing it well. Intuition integrates the left and right brain functions. This can help to give you a more complete perspective on issues. It can also help in better decision-making and improve physical, mental, and emotional health. Intuition is also a means of creative self-expression, especially in the world of art, music, and literature. Scientists, business professionals, and entrepreneurs also follow hunches and gut feelings.

Intuition is ultimately a connection to the subconscious mind. This is how the conscious and unconscious mind communicate. Intuition lives in the present. Therefore, the key to increasing your intuition is to stay present. You begin by listening, by learning to trust your gut feelings and hunches. Pay more attention and be more aware. Everyone has a sense of intuition, though it is often drowned out by the daily demands of time and energy. International Spiritual Teacher Sonia Choquette says, "Your sixth sense should be your first sense."

Yet we are not necessarily taught to take our intuition seriously. Meditation is a tool to strengthen our intuition, a way of focusing attention on our subconscious voice by limiting distraction and allowing the mind to become more aware of intuitive information. Both require a quieting of the mind to listen more clearly to our inner voice and best instincts. The more we begin to gain self-control, and control of our thoughts, the more likely we are able to respond to our intuition and our inner voice.

Personal growth comes alive when we learn to listen to our intuition. We can begin to create a cellular memory of responding internally rather than externally and create a new habit of response. So often we respond without thinking. But are we responding *well* without thinking? Are our impulses and instincts what we hope for? Are we responding with integrity? Do we have regret or are we satisfied with our outcomes? This is how we know ourselves and accept the way we are. We can have a positive effect on our habits, responses, and reactions to things. The better we learn to do this, the more intuitively we learn to respond in a more useful, beneficial manner.

Our intuition knows our spirit, our talents, gifts, and purpose. We often forget to notice our specific abilities, blocking us from reaching our full potential. When we awaken ourselves to who we are and not just what we do, we have more to offer and use less energy to do so. Life can become effortless at times, saving our energy for when we really need it, instead of leaking our energy in a mindless, wasteful way. Our cells have a memory and our minds can be trained. Your intuition is available; just begin by paying more attention.

Your intuition assists you in the process of living a life that matters and guiding others to do so, as well. When you need stress relief and you are not sure how to get it, your intuition knows you need fun and laughter. It thrives on self-care. It knows it is not self-indulgent to take good care of your needs. It knows you are worthy of the life you choose. Life requires balance. Quiet down and just begin to notice and listen.

Allow logic to help balance and refine your intuition. As your intuition develops, so does your awareness of cognitive messages, auditory information, visual images, and physical sensations that provide meaningful information about past, present, or future realities.

Mara M. Zimmerman

Intuition versus Intelligence

Figuring out what is really your intuition and not the rational mind or something else is a learning process that takes trial and error. Your inner knowing comes first from your instincts, second your intellect, and third from your intuition. Instincts have a higher intelligence that come from the past and allow you to survive. Intuition comes from an even higher place that simply just knows and does not require logic. Intellect uses logic to assess the world around you. Use your intellect for the right purpose. The intellect is great at rationalizing so check in with your conscience, which is your judgment of the intellect that distinguishes right from wrong. It is the complex of ethical and moral principles that controls or inhibits the actions or thoughts of an individual. Your conscience is there to serve you with an inhibiting sense of what is prudent and wise in practical affairs, and guiding you to be attentive and careful for providing for the future.

Intuition and intellect are both strategies for problem solving, although logic and intellect are often taught to be the superior method. Logic is not better, just different. Logic is necessary and important in science, math, and even daily life. Yet, so is intuition. Great scientist, doctors, mathematicians, and great spiritual and world leaders will use both logic and intuition. Both strategies have their advantages and apply to different situations. Sometimes we need one or the other, and other times we need both. Intuition functions on different level than logic and intellect. It operates on events, not theories.

Psyche and The Self: East meets West

Eastern

In Vedic times, the yogis investigated the deepest nature of the human being. They developed a philosophy on human existence on material, psychological, and spiritual levels. Ayurveda, meaning the science of life, is the natural healing system and medical tradition of yoga. Ayurveda is as much psychological as it is physical. We can begin to understand ourselves as a whole and find balance through the body, mind, ego, intellect, and Self.

Body

The body is seen as a great generator of electrical energy. All of the cells in the body are kept alive by energy. Nerves connect the brain and the spine with the organs and the seven major energy centers run along the spine.

Mind

The mind is the combination of brain, breath, nerves, sense organs, and work organs that function as a unit. The mind is the tool of consciousness, which enables perception through the senses. It uses the brain to process the signals that are coming through in the senses, but the mind is not the product of the brain. This is proven by observing organisms that have no real brain but still have a mind that enables them to sense changes in the environment.

The mind is described as very active and associative, as it can jump from present to past and from one situation to another. The activity of the mind is seen as closely associated with the pattern of breathing. Therefore, by practicing better breathing, and calming the breath, the mind can also become calm.

Ego

The Vedas describe ego as the illusion that the "I" exists as a separate individual being. The ego is seen as the one that assumes responsibility for the body and identifies with the body. Where the mind is daring, the ego is afraid. When problems arise in the body, the ego becomes alert. The more danger there is, the stronger the ego becomes. When one has to fight or struggle, or even compete, the ego strengthens, for survival, and one learns from their struggle how to be strong. The part of the ego that gives this strength is called will.

Intellect

Intellect is the tool of consciousness that contains knowledge. Intellect carries with it the past and the present and also speculates and considers the future. Intellect helps the ego with advice, but the final decision comes from the ego. The mind and intellect serve ego.

Self

The Self is considered the true nature of one's being and the divine spark of consciousness within each of us. It acknowledges the soul, is bliss and untouched by any of the events happening around us.

In deep sleep, deep concentration, and meditation, the mind, ego, and intellect are inactive. Therefore, deep sleep and meditation are similar. The major difference is that in sleep we are not conscious and in meditation we remain conscious.

Understanding Eastern views of the psyche helps us to thread our thinking with Western views. Modern ideas and facts assist us in one way and ancient ideas and facts assist us in other ways. Together we gain knowledge and insights and can learn more about the world and ourselves. Western scientific thought has gained knowledge from the East and even expanded upon ancient ideas and proved theories and answered questions from the past not answered before or answered from a new or different point of view. This may be useful as you approach your meditation in that you may learn something that assists you in reaching your needs and goals.

Western

The id, ego and superego are the three aspects that make up the structural model of our psyche. According to Freud, their activity and interaction describe our mental life.

Id

The id, our instinct, is the part of the psyche residing in the unconscious that is the source of instinctive impulses that seek satisfaction in accordance with the pleasure principle and are modified by the ego and superego before they are given overt expression. The id is an important part of our personality because as newborns, it allows us to get our basic needs met.

The id wants whatever feels good at the time, with no consideration of the reality of the situation. It does not care about the needs of anyone else, only its own satisfaction. As a child interacts more with the world, the second part of the personality begins to develop – the ego.

Ego

The ego is defined as the 'I' or Self of any person thinking, feeling, willing, and distinguishing itself from the selves of others and from objects of its thought. Do not confuse ego with your true self. The Higher Self knows that the ego is like a good pet. It has its place but must be trained.

Another definition of ego in psychoanalysis is the part of the psychic apparatus that experiences and reacts to the outside world and thus mediates between the primitive drives, the id or our basic instincts, and the demands of the social and physical environment. Ego is also related to your self-esteem or self-image. We all have ego, but is it a healthy balanced ego? Egotism is defined as conceit: self-importance.

Superego

The superego is the ethical component of the personality that provides moral standards by which the ego operates. The superegos criticisms, prohibitions, and inhibitions form a person's conscience, and its positive aspirations and ideals represent one's idealized self-image. In a healthy person, the ego is the strongest so that it can satisfy the needs of the id, not upset the superego, our conscience and moral fiber, and still take into consideration the reality of the situation – not an easy job. If the id becomes too strong, impulses and self-gratification take over. If the superego becomes too strong, the person is driven by rigid morals, is judgmental and unbending in his or her interactions with the world.

Meditation can address the ego as well as the Self in a healthy way. Today, we are aware that we are filled with emotions but we often mask our symptoms. Meditation is a means for acknowledging these symptoms and gaining some empowerment in our approach to them. It helps us to allow ourselves the knowledge that the feelings and emotions we have are valid and serve as radar for what we need. We can notice our physical ailments and honor them so they do not progress and worsen, addressing them with confidence and courage by seeing ourselves more clearly and finding more physical and emotional health and inner calm. This is possible by simply finding more peace and quiet and finding a focus that is more mindful.

Mind-Brain Connection

Are your brain and mind one and the same? The mind vs. brain debate has been going on since before Aristotle. He and Plato argued that the soul housed intelligence or wisdom and that it was not placed directly in the physical body. Descartes identified the mind with consciousness and self-awareness itself, with an ability to distinguish itself from the brain. But he still called the brain the seat of intelligence. In yoga science, the mind is considered an element and therefore non-physical by nature. It is said to retain thought faster than the speed of light and retains all experience whether consciously addressed by the thinker or not. It contains the aura, the energy body, and communicates the language of feeling.

The mind has a profound effect on the energy level of the physical body, which temporarily houses the mind. When your mind changes, your brain changes too. Fleeting thoughts and feelings can leave lasting marks on your brain. What flows through your mind shapes your brain. Thus, you can use your mind to change your brain for your benefit. When your mind is happy and wise it has an effect on your brain. Meditation can help activate these brain states when you learn to control your thoughts. Strengthening your brain states can help you rewire your brain and bring about better well-being.

Your brain, shaped by the mind, interacts with the other systems of your body. In a larger sense, your mind is made by your brain, body, the world around you, and human nature. We can simplify this by saying the brain is the basis of the mind. The mind and brain interact with each other so profoundly that they are best referred to and understood as a single, codependent, mind-brain system.

Since no one knows exactly how the brain and the mind interact, we can use this idea for a step towards meditation, contemplating the possibilities. Meditation has a potent effect on the mind and therefore your brain. It is useful to understand the power and possibilities. The nervous system is affected through the breath and good posture. The limbic system is affected in the brain when you find calm and has an influence on your behavior, thoughts, and emotions. The medulla oblongata, located at the lowest part of the brainstem, controls functions such as respiration, heart rate, and digestion. Meditation can improve your breathing which can recharge this area of your brain.

Meditation has been scientifically tested on the brains of monks and those who spend much time in meditation. Results show powerful and unusual brainwave activity affecting and integrating the mind and experiences of greater happiness, love, and wisdom. Simply being mindful is a passive form of meditation and has a positive effect on the brain. There are two hemispheres of the brain, referred to as the right brain and the left brain. The left is associated with analytical, rational, and logical processing while the right is associated with abstract thought, emotions, creativity, and intuition. Practicing mindfulness and being more present while creating more focus and reducing thinking, brings more calm and assists in a shift from the left to the right brain, allowing for more whole brain and holistic thinking.

Hemispheres of the Brain

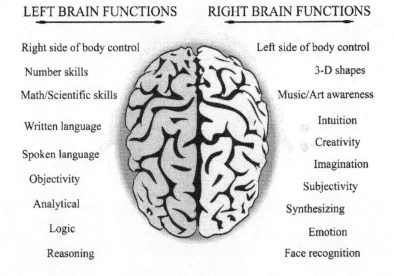

LEFT BRAIN FUNCTIONS	RIGHT BRAIN FUNCTIONS
Right side of body control	Left side of body control
Number skills	3-D shapes
Math/Scientific skills	Music/Art awareness
Written language	Intuition
Spoken language	Creativity
	Imagination
Objectivity	Subjectivity
Analytical	Synthesizing
Logic	Emotion
Reasoning	Face recognition

Understanding more about your brain as well as your mind is a step in the process of meditation. An awakening mind means an awakening brain. Both benefit from the gifts of meditation.

Understanding Eastern and Western thoughts on the psyche can help us gain a better understanding of our self. Any time we are gaining a better understanding of ourselves, we are taking a step in the process of meditation.

CHAPTER 5

THE MIND-BODY CONNECTION

*"Breathing in, I calm body and mind. Breathing
out, I smile." -Thich Nhat Hanh*

The mind and body are easy to see as separate entities, yet it is just as simple to see them as a whole. It is not a leap to *make* this connection. The leap is to notice and pay more attention to it. So often we rely on the body's amazing abilities that are unconscious and involuntary that we do not bother to make certain connections. Our body is doing one thing and our mind another. Bringing them into synchronicity is a step in the meditation process. Becoming more aware is, as well. When we are more mindful of our body and mind connection we are naturally more present.

Bringing the opportunity for well-being by noticing our symptoms and needs more readily we can create more vitality. Our minds wander away from our body's needs until we are forced to notice. We can prevent issues by staying more present and noticing needs before problems arise. We sometimes pay more attention to one or the other. Our body can be a distraction from our mind and our mind can distract us from our body. The breath is the link between the two. We can begin to notice those moments when our body and mind are in disagreement. Your body needs to physically be somewhere like work, or a difficult parenting time period, or something else undesired. These can be moments of opportunity to meditate. You do not need to be engaged in an ancient or popular meditation technique or for a specific amount of time. Bringing calm and mindfulness to a stressful or beautiful situation even for a moment are the beginning stages of meditation and can bring many benefits. Rather than being stressed in the moment or missing the beauty, a mindful moment can bring peace and inner calm that may or may not expand into further outcome. Every moment counts as a possibility.

The main problem with the mind is that because it makes interpretations from memory, it does not deal as well with the new and unknown. The mind has no reference for it. Your mind and body both have memories – some useful, some not so much. Your mind's memory encompasses the memory of all the cells in your body. You can create new mental memories by cultivating healthy relationships and finding and giving love. You can create new, more positive muscle memory by healthy exercising and good posture. Yoga is a great activity and discipline for this purpose – harnessing the mind and moving through physical challenges, balancing, stretching, and strengthening, focusing on the breath, and creating less thinking and more action. Yoga helps you learn when to push the mind and body and when to back off.

Self-Judgment

Notice when you judge your body and compare it to others. Be aware of how you view your body and how your mind interprets that. In a culture promoting fitness superficially, yet providing much room for gluttony, it can be confusing and often unreachable for someone to tap into the best look and size for themselves and have their mind accept and agree with it. You may look great, but do you feel great? You may feel great, but do you look great? This duality of personal health can be confusing. This may be a time when your mind and body disconnect: "I need to be this weight so I won't listen to my mind's needs." or "I have to get this work done so I won't listen to my body's needs."

All over the world there are differences in how the body and mind are viewed. The common factor is that no matter how you view or even treat your body and mind, they are still connected. It is the stress that is put on your body and mind that matters. Meditation acknowledges this. The question is if you choose to honor your mind–body connection and work at integrating them. In a world of superficiality, where especially women but men as well are so often viewed as physical objects, it can be difficult to have a healthy body image and mindset. Beauty comes from within, yet our minds are often thrown off by what we see around us. Advertising, commercialism, and materialism have their place yet sometimes overwhelm.

We should aspire to be our best in both our minds and bodies. Seeing yourself from a healthy standpoint is important and so is knowing what your body and mind need. That way, you will naturally maintain a better or appropriate body weight. You will learn to enjoy simple pleasures and not feel guilty. You can embrace good health and know that your body and mind will be a reflection of it. We often take advantage of our body's systems, paying little attention to our internal and visceral needs, relying heavily on our superficial needs and then struggling to find a balance. Some are born with great looking bodies and great thinking minds. Others have more obstacles and challenges in these areas. Having more body weight in some cultures is considered good fortune and a sign of abundance. In other cultures more body weight is an avenue for shame and self-loathing. We need to be realistic. What are my genetics? How do I approach my health? How do I see myself and how am I in reality? A healthy mindset will be a good basis and help set the foundation for a healthy body. Vise versa, a healthy body will be a basis for a healthy mindset. Sitting in meditation can help us consider this. Also, finding appropriate activities to strengthen our minds, looking into topics that matter and bring meaning to life, and finding purpose in what we do. Do I do things for the wrong reasons? Do I reach for the right foods? Do I enjoy life? Am I happy in my body? Am I peaceful in my mind? Am I complete?

A Healthy Mind–Body Connection

Meditation has a great effect on the nervous system, strengthening the mind-body connection. Your spine connects your body to your brain, and your posture affects your state of mind, "mood" or "outlook". Chiropractic, a form of natural medicine and hands on healing, addresses the spine directly with the goal of spinal alignment for increased brain-body health and wellness. When messages are flowing freely and optimally from the body to the brain and your nervous system is functioning at its best, you naturally have an improved state of mind. States of mind also affect the heart, your emotional center. A healthy state of mind can assist you in getting along with others, keep you alert and energized, solve problems more peacefully, be secure, and calm, compassionate, empathetic and kind. A dull state of mind, on the other hand, will weaken these abilities. A "monkey mind," or mind that is unsettled and has too much activity, will create an obstacle in this area as well. An alternating or oscillating mind is unfocused and unclear. A single-pointed attentive mind will strengthen abilities and lead you toward a highest state of restrained consciousness.

When we simply sit with good posture we set the intention for an improved state of mind, and therefore an improved mind-body connection. In this way, we allow our systems to work together. Choose activities you enjoy whenever possible. Forcing your body to do activities that your mind is complaining about is not harmonious.

Taking too much time for your mind's attention span and ability to focus can be depleting and create negative thinking. Begin to notice when you are exercising or resting how your mind is responding. Notice when you are being mindful, how your body is responding. Do not ignore important messages that your mind and body are sending each other such as symptoms and emotions. Mind over matter, the use of willpower to overcome physical and emotional obstacles is a great skill under certain circumstances, and has its time and place. We can also learn to regard important intuitive messages and disregard sabotaging thoughts. The more you do this, the easier it gets. Develop a mind-body routine that you look forward to. Meditation is key since it addresses both the body and the mind. It does not require too much: good posture, mindfulness of breathing, and a temporary distraction from thoughts.

Meditation may have a positive effect on the nervous system as a whole as you develop the skill of sitting and standing and moving in general in good posture, better connecting the spine and the brain for clearer messages, breathing slower and in a more conscious and balanced manner. The body and mind are complex, but by simply bringing it all back to our posture and breathing we can get back to the basics, creating a good foundation and a cellular memory that keeps us in check. Good posture can also set the tone for self-confidence. Learning more about our complexities need not be overwhelming, just informative. Take in what comes naturally and sit with the idea that you can keep it simple and just breathe. Our bodies and minds are sacred. How we treat them matters. How we treat others and ourselves matters. When we remember to honor our bodies, our thoughts and the breath that gives us life, we are in the process of meditation. Our mindfulness slows us down; this is a simple way to honor our self.

Minding your body and how it affects your mind, as well as minding your mind and how it affects your body are a basis for meditation. You need not understand exactly how all of the systems interact to treat yourself well.

Keeping good hygiene, caring for your inside and outside is important – washing, brushing, exercising, eating, resting, sleeping, breathing, and even sitting. This is also true of your mind. Be curious, keeping your mind clear, quiet, open, giving it exercise and rest. Learn new things, create good habits, care for yourself and others – these are all steps in the meditation process. Your morals, ethics, and the way in which you value your body and mind matter and are relevant when you meditate. They bring meaning and self-awareness of the way you show up in the world. Contemplating this connection of how you treat the parts of yourself and how you integrate is absolutely a step in the process of meditation.

Accessing Your Mind-Body Connection in Difficult Situations

As your mind "awakens," so does your ability to access better emotions. When we cultivate more sublime and peaceful states, we are better able to alleviate the physical or emotional suffering we experience in everyday life. Worry and fear are something all human beings share, and when we awaken to this reality, it helps us to feel less alone and therefore more connected.

Buddha described qualities of the mind that alleviate suffering. For example, the Sanskrit word *metta,* which means loving-kindness or even "friendliness". This is simply an idea of wishing others well, even those you do not get along with or do not keep in your direct circle of life. *Chesed* is the Hebrew word for love and kindness and loving-kindness creates compassion for you and for others. Wish for others what you would wish for yourself.

Knowing how to set good and appropriate boundaries for your body and your mind, and aspiring to keep a healthy state of mind even when feeling judgmental, can help keep you integrated and safe. This is where your intuition can come in handy – gaining insights in how to approach difficult situations that will give you the most ideal outcome, knowing what you will need to function and cope. Others will not always need what you need. Others will not always honor you. So simply remaining in a healthy mindset, keeping your distance physically and using common sense, yet sending well-wishes mindfully, will be good for you and set a good example. Your body and mind need good boundaries. They will not tolerate neglect for too long. So catch yourself when you let things go and course correct whenever possible. Your body and mind will drift from discipline and health from time to time, but simply notice sooner, and bring them back to wholeness and center.

Meditation is such a gift in this area. Your body and mind will need attention. You will forget sometimes. You will have problems with dear friends and family members. This can be quite challenging and create many emotional and even physical obstacles and problems. Stay connected to yourself and your needs and keep your distance when necessary. Yet do not bother to carry the negativity. Not everyone evolves at the same pace. People will have differences – that is human nature. Finding some inner peace is a part of the process for inner healing and self-worth.

Meditation is a guide. Taking pause. Allow your heart to be a bridge between your body and mind. Your heart is a wonderful radar: "This is good for me it brings me loving-kindness," or "This is not so good for me it does not bring me loving-kindness."

Do not force your body or mind into any situation that does not bring loving-kindness whenever possible. When impossible to avoid, set good boundaries, be discerning and be the catalyst for loving-kindness. Avoid things that bring damage to your body and mind. What you do not do is just as important as what you do. So, eat well, drink enough water, exercise well, think well, and rest well. Give and receive well, learn well, and clean well. Be serious, be disciplined, and be practical and wise. Be focused, be patient, pay attention, and treat yourself and others well. Have courage; stand up for others and also for yourself. Remember to let go, even lighten up and have some fun. Laugh. It is good for your body and mind to simply smile. Practicing loving-kindness for others and also for you, your body, heart and mind, is a step in the process of meditation.

We need our bodies and our minds to remain healthy during our aging process. Physical, mental, and emotional balance is key to a high quality of life and independent living. Grasping this as soon as possible will benefit you as you age. Treating your body and mind with care and acknowledging the benefits of prevention will go a long way. Meditation can assist you in noticing what you need and do not need, relieve stress in your body and mind, and prevent symptoms from escalating. Symptoms are a good way to listen to your body and mind. Ignoring signs and symptoms can become problematic. Learn that by listening, our bodies and minds tell us what we need and are a path toward healing.

CHAPTER 6

THE ANATOMY OF THE ENERGY BODY

"Life and the sun are so intimately connected." -Kabbalah

Learning about aspects of your body's energy offers the possibility of healing and growth. Understanding your mind's connection to your brain, heart, and physical body, and your mental and emotional states, help you harness your thought process through meditation.

We can begin to address the idea of our energy body by simply checking in with our energy levels, understanding we have an energy body. We all have energy. This does not require a belief system. Check in with your energy body by simply noting how you are feeling. Do you have a little or a lot of energy to face the day? Notice this on a physical level. Is your body tired or ready to go? Notice on an emotional level. Do you feel emotionally sound or drained? Notice on a mental level. Is your thinking sharp or dull? Do you have the energy you need to do your work and to be with your family? Do you waste your energy?

Meditation can help you build internal energy by learning to store your energy so you have reserves for when you need it. Getting proper nutrition fuels your body with energy. Breathing properly and optimally and getting the right amount of exercise also fuels your energy. If you eat poorly, over exercise, or do not exercise at all, you may feel lazy and drained. Exercises for your mind keep you sharp so you do not have to overthink unnecessarily. Begin to notice your own energy levels and you will become more aware of your energy body. This is a step in the process of meditation.

In this chapter, I will delve into several ways to uncover our energy bodies. Western medicine and science may not spend as much time healing or understanding our energy body as in Eastern traditions, but that does not mean that we cannot gain some knowledge about it to complement what we already know. While they originate from different traditions, these models all can be helpful in discovering who we are and what we need. Some may feel more relevant to you than others, so read on to see which best resonate.

Subtle Bodies

The term subtle energy, described in a number of Eastern traditions, refers to the force field surrounding all living things. It comprises the aura and the seven layers of energy known as subtle bodies. These affect our physical well-being, our emotional stability, and our mental clarity. An aura is the atmosphere or quality that surrounds and is generated by a person, place, or thing. Your aura encompasses all of your energy body. People have an "aura" or energy about them. You may notice how others show up. Their energy may be intense or overbearing. Or their energy reflects kindness and generosity. Your energy reflects your personality.

Your physical, mental, and emotional states are all interconnected and affect one another. We are not just a body. Nor are we just our state of mind. We are not fragmented in truth, just in thought. So be mindful and careful of your thoughts and be good to your body. These are all a part of the process.

Chakras Overview

Chakra is a Sanskrit word that means wheel of energy. The chakras reflect your light or energy body. Originating in India, they are the ancient models that describe the human energy system. When they are in balance, open and cleared, positive energy flows, promoting physical and emotional health.

The chakras stimulate the endocrine organs. The lower chakras are magnetic energy and embrace the feminine as they take in their energy from the earth and immediate environment. They connect us with Mother Earth, family, and community.

The upper chakras are electrical and connected to the masculine as they are primarily concerned with giving energy out through love, communication, healthy attitudes, and inner reflection.

Chakras work interdependent of one another. When one shuts down others will compensate to maintain life force. The chakras are a well-organized system, and our health and wellness depend on active, balanced chakras.

Our chakras develop through our early childhood and continue to develop throughout our lives. So, as you grow and develop physically, mentally, emotionally, or spiritually, you also develop energetically. Knowing a bit about your energy body and considering and contemplating the ways you function energetically, is a step in the meditation process.

As I describe and introduce the qualities of the seven major chakras, I have included an affirmation and a mantra for each. Affirmations and mantras are a simple way to approach meditation. They give a focus for quiet sitting and mindfulness, allowing for distraction from thought and creating a positive mental attitude. These may be said aloud or silently in the mind.

Knowing who you are and beginning to consider, contemplate, and meditate on qualities and aspects of yourself may bring more awareness, insight, balance, and healing. As you read, you may notice some things about your personality – some difficult and some wonderful.

Also included are the main colors and gemstones that are associated with each chakra. This may be useful to you as you are learning to heighten your awareness of how things affect you. As well, there are certain glands/hormones that are linked with each energy center. This may be interesting to you when considering your general or specific health and wellness as you approach meditation.

Meditation can assist you in your awareness and flow of your energy, and learning about the energy systems can help you see more clearly the benefit you can have on your own energy body. Meditation can be a useful time to address your energy body even for a simple distraction from your thoughts. Your inner voice will chatter on yet you can contemplate your energy body all the while. Visualizing your chakras assists your mind and body to connect.

The Seven Major Chakras

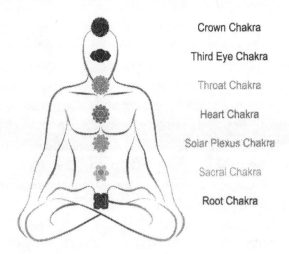

Crown Chakra

Third Eye Chakra

Throat Chakra

Heart Chakra

Solar Plexus Chakra

Sacral Chakra

Root Chakra

The 7 Major Chakras run along your spine beginning at the base and move up to the crown of your head.

1. Root Chakra or Muladhara in Sanskrit, mula meaning root.
    - Located at the base of your spine and extends down your legs and feet.
    - Associated with the color red.
    - Associated with the kidneys and adrenal glands and affects your vitality, immunity and energy levels.
    - The Root Chakra reflects upon your foundation, grounding, survival and purpose. It reflects qualities of self-management, responsibility, personal power, patience, stability, security, presence and inner strength.

Affirmation for the First Chakra: "I am beautiful because I am."

Mantra or sound for the First Chakra: "Lam"

Gemstone: Garnet, Smoky Quartz, Ruby

2. Sacral Chakra, in Sanskrit Svadhisthana, meaning one's own base.
   - Located just below the navel.
   - It is associated with the color orange.
   - Glandular connection is to the reproductive glands/ organs. The ovaries in women and testes in men are your reproductive glands and they control sexual development.
   - The Sacral Chakra reflects your general health, inner child, healthy sexuality, relationship to your body, fertility, intimacy, bonding, management of finances, and spiritual nature. It reflects qualities of knowing you are enough, enjoyment in life, taking action and having good boundaries.

Affirmation for the Second Chakra: "I make healthy choices."

Mantra or sound for the Second Chakra: "Vam"

Gemstone: Carnelian, Tigers Eye, Topaz

3. Solar Plexus Chakra, in Sanskrit Manipura, meaning jewel.
   - Located at your center, above the navel and below the sternum.
   - It is associated with the color yellow.
   - It is associated with the pancreas which is a dual functioning organ/gland located in the abdomen that affects immunity and the digestive system.
   - The Solar Plexus Chakra reflects your personal identity, your inner fire, relationships, self-worth, self-esteem and ability to be centered, balanced and confident.

Affirmation for Third Chakra: "I am calm and capable."

Mantra or sound for the Third Chakra: "Ram"

Gemstone: Citrine, Amber

4. Heart Chakra, in Sanskrit Anahata, meaning unstruck.
    - Located in the heart center and extends to your arms and hands.
    - It is associated with the colors green and pink.
    - The glandular connection is the thymus gland, located in the upper chest, behind the sternum and in front of the heart. It is associated with the immune system and is most active in childhood.
    - The Heart Chakra governs the physical heart and the lungs. Qualities reflect self-love, unconditional love, unity, peace, forgiveness, kindness, compassion, empathy, and acceptance.

Affirmation for Fourth Chakra: "I give and receive love in a healthy way."

Mantra or sound for the Fourth Chakra: "Yam"

Gemstone: Emerald, Peridot, Jade, Rose Quartz

5. Throat Chakra, in Sanskrit Vishuddha meaning purification.
    - Located at the internal and external throat.
    - Associated with the color turquoise.
    - The glandular connection is to the thyroid and parathyroid glands. The thyroid gland is the largest in the neck and is located in the front below the skin and muscle layers. It functions to regulate the body's metabolism.
    - The Throat Chakra differentiates humans from all other life forms and gives us the power to express ourselves. Qualities reflect a person's will, ability to communicate, personal integrity, creativity and ability to speak their truth.

Affirmation for the Fifth Chakra: "I say what I mean and mean what I say."

Mantra or sound for the Fifth Chakra: "Ham"

Gemstone: Turquoise, Aquamarine

6. Brow Chakra, in Sanskrit Ajna, meaning to perceive, to know.
   • Located between the eyebrows.
   • Associated with the color dark blue.
   • The glandular association is the pituitary gland, often referred to as the "master gland" due to its role in controlling other hormone glands. It sits behind the bridge of the nose and below the base of the brain. This is the center for the "third eye", the center for intuition. It controls growth and development.
   • The Brow Chakra reflects qualities of a strong and independent mind and intellect, imagination, inner knowing, intuition and wisdom.

Affirmation for the Sixth Chakra: "I learn from my past and listen to my intuition in the present to help guide me toward my future."

Mantra or sound for the Sixth Chakra: "Om"

Gemstone: Lapis Lazuli, Sapphire

7. The Crown Chakra, in Sanskrit Sahasrara, meaning thousand-petaled.
   • Located at the top of skull.
   • It is associated with the color purple.
   • The glandular association is the pineal gland, which is located at the top of the head, between the two

hemispheres of the brain. It affects sleep patterns and is associated with perception. We activate this gland when we meditate.

- The Crown Chakra reflects qualities of grace, beauty, serenity, wholeness, Oneness with all that is and connection with your Higher Self. The Higher Self is wise, spiritual by nature, and encompasses all of who you are.

Affirmation for Seventh Chakra: "I am peaceful and connected."

Mantra or sound for the Seventh Chakra: Silence

Gemstone: Amethyst, Purple Fluorite, Diamond

Quartz Crystal: Balancing for all Chakras

Understanding your energy body is a wonderful tool in the process of meditation. It can help you find empowerment, vitality, and establish your life purpose, health and wellness. Begin to notice what works and does not work in your life, what is in balance and out of balance, what is abundant and deficient. Enjoy knowing that you have a say in your health, how you think, what you eat, your level of exercise, your habits, and how you breathe, give, and receive.

The 12 Meridians

According to Chinese medicine, the meridian system is a way to describe the energy distribution system. This helps us to understand how our Qi, Chi, or energy, and blood and bodily fluids, permeate and flow through the body. The individual meridians or channels reflect the notion of carrying, holding, or transporting these throughout the body. While conventional anatomy and physiology do not identify these pathways in a physical sense, the way, for instance, that blood vessels can be identified, it is useful to consider the meridian system from an energetic standpoint.

There are 12 main meridians throughout the body. They access all parts of the body. Like highways, they can be mapped. They flow within the body and not on the surface. Meridians exist in corresponding pairs, and each meridian has many acupuncture and acupressure points along its path. They can be understood as a process rather than a structure. This is useful to understand in the process of meditation when we are increasing our awareness of who we are and how we function. Six channels traverse each limb and each meridian is a Yin-Yang pair that corresponds to different organs. Each must be in balance with one another to maintain health and homeostasis and be disease free. Excess in one area stimulates a deficiency in another; deficiency in one area stimulates excess in another. Along the meridians are many points that may be used to help unblock energy. Your hands, feet, and ears have pressure points that reflect on the whole body. A simple massage or putting pressure on a certain point can have a calming and healing effect.

Pressure Points in Feet

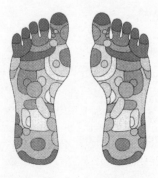

Inner Clock

The Meridian Clock or Meridian Flow Wheel is a tool that acknowledges our inner clock and inner knowing. It allows us to take more notice and be more aware of our symptoms and why they are relevant. Symptoms are the body and mind's way of telling us things about ourselves and guiding us back to balance. This clock illustrates the flow of energy through the meridians during the 24 hours of the day. Acupuncturists use this information diagnostically. It is a handy and informative tool in self-awareness and self-realization. If you are prone to waking the same time each night or have a low time during the day, this clock may provide information and insight into some aspect of your health.

When beginning to meditate, as you are noticing more about your own energy, begin to notice your inner clock and how it is working with the clock of your daily life and responsibilities. It can be helpful as you begin and expand upon your meditation process. What times of day are you at your best? What times are you at a low? When do you need a snack or a break? Do you go to sleep easily? Do you need an alarm to wake in the morning? Do you already have a good rhythm? Begin to take notice.

Sefirot-Attributes of the Physical and Metaphysical Realms

Kabbalah teaches the Ten Sefirot. Originally in Hebrew, they reveal attributes that interact with each other and the outside world. The Hebrew letters are also a means for contemplation and meditation. The Sefirot offer insight into the soul, universal energy and our energy body. They are the ten creative forces that intervene between the infinite and our created world. They offer insights toward healing and the Self. They give a viewpoint relevant to our energy and are therefore a good step in the meditation process. Metaphysics philosophically aims to deal with the nature of the mind and the nature of being. Metaphysical realms go beyond the physical and into the spiritual.

The Sefirot are interconnected, which means that each Sefirah contains within it all of the others. This exists both within the Self and the outer world. Understanding these aspects, contemplating, visualizing and exploring them, individually and as a whole, is a step in the process of meditation. This also relates to the notion that our mind, body, and spirit are all interconnected.

The Ten Sefirot has insights to offer. They have colors associated with them as well as numbers. They are often shown in a diagram in the form of a tree, as in a tree of life. There are varying interpretations and perspectives. I have described an interpretation that may be useful as you begin meditation. It may bring you more self-awareness or help you to visualize your energy body at times of stress or in the stillness of meditation as a means to create inner peace and new ways of thinking.

The Ten Sefirot

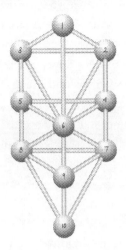

Ten Sefirot as they relate to our energy or "light body:"

1. Keter-Crown and Ayin-Nothingness. The mind is a place where nothing exists. This reflects a state of meditation of the Higher Self and connection to the universe. It is central to the body and produces and affects all other nine Sefirah. It is located at the top of the head, like a crown. Associated with the color white, like a blinding light.

2. Chokhmah-Wisdom. This is a point of higher wisdom or awareness that proceeds from nothingness. Knowing is the origin of thought and mental energy. It channels the pure energy of Keter into a kind of energy that can be put to use in the form of the intellect. Located at the temples and brow, it represents masculine energy on right side of the body and temple and the right hemisphere of the brain. Associated with all colors.

3. Binah-Understanding. A partner to Chokhmah that represents feminine energy. Located at the brow and temples, it is on the left side of body and the left

hemisphere of the brain. It refines the pure intellect of the Chokhmah into more specific thoughts and ideas. It receives the seeds of Chokhmah and is the "womb that conceives" the Sefirot. It is considered the mother of the Sefirot and from her comes all created being. Associated with the colors yellow and green.

4. Chesed-Love and kindness. Love, kindness and mercy are the first offspring, so to speak, of Binah and the first of the emotional attributes, the beginning of emotional energy. An act of loving-kindness given freely without restraint, it represents the right side, more specifically the right arm and is the masculine emotional energy. Associated with the colors white and silver.

5. Gevurah-Strength and Din-Judgment. Knowing our own strength and restrictive power and showing discipline and restraint with our capacity. It represents the left side and the left arm, the feminine and further development of emotional energy. It imposes judgment to harness energy. Chesed and Gevurah must balance one another. In other words, love and kindness must balance strength and knowing. Associated with the colors red and gold.

6. Tiferet–Beauty. This represents and integrates the balance of Chesed, loving-kindness and Gevurah, strength and knowing. It is a reflection of compassion and the harmony of giving and receiving. It is central in the body, the chest and torso. Associated with the colors yellow and purple.

7. Netzach-Victory and Endurance. This represents the right side and the right leg. It also represents an undefined spiritual energy and the ability to overcome obstacles. Associated with the color light pink.

8. Hod-Splendor. This is associated with the left side and the left leg. It begins to represent the material world and the world of sensation – smells, sights, sound, taste and all senses. It gives Netzach its undefined energy form

through the senses and assists in acknowledging your life purpose. Associated with the color dark pink.

9. Yesod-Foundation. This is in the middle of the body at the hips and represents procreation and grounding. It balances Netzach, victory, and Hod, splendor, and channels energy through the final Sefirah. Associated with the color orange.

10. Malkhut-Kingdom and Shekhinah-Presence. At the base of and central to the body, it is associated with the feet, the spine and at times the mouth and breath. It is connected to the created world, the moon and earth. It represents self-expression and gathers all of the energies from the other nine Sefirah and transmits them throughout the physical human world and human body. Associated with the color blue.

In a patriarchal world, it is always refreshing when the balance and importance of the feminine is acknowledged, celebrated, and embraced. By understanding more about our energy body and the energy of our true nature, we leave the patriarch's limited view and expand our mind and consciousness into the matriarch, her importance and relevance. We may then realize that they both exist in balance, having strengths and weaknesses relevant to us all. This realization is a beautiful and profound way to begin increasing your awareness and personal growth and may assist in the process of meditation.

*   *   *

Some of the different energy systems I've described overlap and have similarities, while others differ. This may be useful when you are interpreting what your needs are and what works for you. Like the chakras, the meridians and the energy body as a whole, the Sefirot exist separately and together at once. This is also true of your brain, mind, body, and emotions. The Sefirot is considered a tree of life yet the tree begins at the crown and draws its energy from the universe and the divine. In the material world humans begin their knowledge at the bottom and move closer to the divine as we learn and grow. In chakra development, humans are also beginning with the root and their connection to the earth first and resonating with the upper chakras and their crown as they become more aware and grow throughout life.

This is a profound ancient wisdom that has always existed whether we acknowledge it or not. We can separate things yet they still exist as a whole. Many cultures have embraced this idea, and it is a foundation and basis for meditation technique. You need not fully grasp any one or all of these concepts, yet they still exist. If you begin your process toward meditation with the basic understanding that your thoughts seem to exist separate from but are actually a part of your whole self, and you simply sit and notice your thoughts, you are becoming more self-aware. This is an important step in the process of meditation.

Why is it useful to learn more about our energy, mind, and body and their connection when learning to meditate? This can assist in setting healthy boundaries and tune you more in to your needs. It can help create sensitivity to yourself that you may need to remain healthy and balanced as you age. It also sheds light on how interconnected your emotions are with your energy body. Your energy body is an aspect of meditation because it is a part of you. If learning about your energy body does not resonate, then notice the areas that do. Become more aware in the areas that you are drawn to – mind, body or spirit – and bring that with you to your meditation process.

All of the energy body systems are as important as Western views of the body's anatomy. Just like the mind, brain and nervous systems, the energy body has a great effect on our health and well-being. Even if you do not apply these ideas, we are learning to grow and expand our minds so we may better see what resonates with each of us and what does not. This way we can approach the process of meditation in an individual manner, knowing a bit more what we need and do not need, what serves and interests us, and what moves us into action.

Meditation is about expanding the mind by first restricting the mind to details that may inspire you to let go without being attached to the outcome. This includes allowing thoughts to come and go without emotional reaction and ups and downs, learning you can create a positive inner environment. Meditation alleviates the need to stop thinking and instead allows thoughts to come and go and replace them with new and more compassionate ones. It means being in the process without expectation.

Basic understanding need not be threatening. When you are first learning something new or different, you can decide if it works for you and realize whether it does or does not, it may for someone else and that either way it still exists. Embracing our personal freedom and allowing others to embrace theirs, is an ultimate step towards peace in the world, inner peace and peace in meditation.

PART III

HOW TO MEDITATE

CHAPTER 7

TYPES OF MEDITATION

*"Look deep into nature, and then you will
understand everything better."*
-Albert Einstein

Meditation is integration: the fragmented parts become one and we
see things as they really are. Meditation is a way of self-transformation
through self-observation. Focus is on deep interconnection
between body and mind. Life becomes characterized by increased
awareness, non-delusion, self-control, and peace.

We all have a physical body with a heart, a mind with an inner
voice, a thinking and multidimensional brain, and a spine and
nervous system. We all have a breath. We all have our own
reasons for exploring meditation. Learning a bit more about it
may help inspire some action without much effort. At the end of
the day, the action we take is the grand result of meditation. Being
more conscious may help us to also gain insight into how to best
care for ourselves and the world around us, as well as learn how
to keep ego at bay while the real unselfish Self evolves and shines.

There are many different types of meditation, ranging from simple
to complicated. It can be helpful to recognize what you respond well

to and what you resist, what helps you to relax and what irritates you, being comfortable in yourself even when things are uncomfortable. There need not be one way of approaching it. Finding the proper technique will help to put your practice into action.

By learning about the different types of meditation, we see that people and cultures have differences and similarities. We can apply what resonates within each of us individually and what brings meaning to our personal practice of meditation. When learning about the different ways to approach your meditation practice, keep in mind what your personal needs are. If you are not sure what you need, begin to take note of what might resonate or what each type is offering.

What do you need?

- Do you need relaxation and stress relief?
- Are you trying to be more mindful and learning to be more present?
- Are you looking to increase your vitality?
- Are you interested in connecting with your inner voice and your intuition?
- Do you just need a break sometimes?
- Struggling with sleep?
- Are you looking for more gratitude, courage or inner strength?
- Are you trying to get more in touch with yourself or connect better in your relationships?
- Do you or someone you know need healing?
- Do you need more clarity, focus or better concentration?
- Are you transitioning in some way, soul searching or on a spiritual journey?
- Are you suffering from grief or illness?
- Managing diet or weight loss?
- Dealing with pain or medication?

- Working on developing your creativity?
- Have career or life ambitions to address?
- Seeking more happiness and a positive state of mind?
- Do you need more emotional stability and inner peace and calm?

The reason you are seeking meditation may help you in choosing your path and type. If you are simply just interested with no other aspiration, any or all may apply. Remember to keep it simple. You do not have to be in over your head. You do not need to understand it all. Learning to sit quietly and be more mindful with a reasonable period of time and approach will suffice. Continue to remind yourself that the process is relevant.

Meditation in Yoga

Yoga is India's gift to the world. It recognizes that the way our bodies and minds work has changed very little over the millennium. Vedanta is an ancient philosophy based on the Vedas, the ancient scriptures of India and is where yoga teachings were first written. Vedanta affirms one's existence, the divinity of the soul and the harmony of religions. A few thousand years ago, the scriptures of India affirmed that 'Truth is One', and that the wise call it by different names.

The Eight Petals or Limbs of Yoga

Yoga, meaning to join or union, aims to connect your body, mind, and spirit. Your breath is the vehicle in which to do so. Yoga addresses your strength, flexibility, balance, core, focus, concentration and ultimately meditation. There are a range of styles to fit different needs and duration and a teacher should be a good fit. Having all of the fundamental postural exercises and movement for your spine to be healthy, yoga addresses your energy and oxygen needs through increasing the quality of your breath.

Yoga is one long breathing exercise. As you move from one posture to the next, or as you remain in one pose and breathe, it is easier to get to know your physical, emotional, and mental needs as you see your physical abilities and limitations. When approached well and wisely, it holds a key to a healthy aging process and quality of life.

Yoga helps us hear our inner voice and increases the mind's ability to focus and observe our self and the world by addressing our strengths and weaknesses, breathing better, having good posture, quieting the mind, noticing emotions, our feelings and our energy levels. Yoga can help us grasp that meditation actually is a process. Even if meditation is the goal and you only reach a certain point, you are still growing and advancing toward it by practicing and building on your mindfulness, personal development, and your approach to your body, mind, and everyday life. Even those who devote their entire life to meditation, which is not most of us, will take these steps. We benefit from every stage in the process:

1. Yama- External ethical disciplines that relate to "the golden rule": do unto others, as you would have them do unto you.
2. Niyama- Internal ethical observances relating to self-discipline, cleanliness and organization. Getting your personal space organized may help organize your thoughts.
3. Asana- Beneficial posture for your spine through yoga poses. Sit and stand in good posture, stretch, strengthen and balance your body. Yoga poses are restorative and create focus as you learn to concentrate and be present. Yoga is a unique form of physical exercise in that the final

pose is a resting pose. When you have completed your exercise, you simply lie down and rest.

4. Pranayama- Breathing techniques and breath control. The Ujjayi, or victorious breath, is a diaphragmatic breath which helps calm the mind and body. It can calm the nervous system and balance the emotions. Take a deep inhalation through the nose and exhale through the nose while constricting your throat muscles. This will sound a bit like the ocean.

5. Pratyahara- Drawing awareness away from our senses. Attention is looking inward.

6. Dharana- Focused attention leads to concentration or unbroken awareness.

Along with yoga poses and focused breathing, counting mala beads are a good exercise for limbs five and six. In ancient times, mala beads were counted (mala is the Sanskrit word for necklace) as a step in the process of meditation. There were generally 108 beads, often seeds collected from local trees. By counting the beads, the mind must stay focused in order to not lose count. Yogis would recite a mantra 108 times in place of counting.

Decreased stress and improved emotional state begins in the initial six stages. The process of relaxing the brain and mind for meditation begins with asana, the physical poses, good posture and pranayama, attention to breathing. This way stress is drained away and the mind and body relax and gain awareness as a whole. This will assist in concentration and help to begin to withdraw your senses for meditation.

7. Dhyana- Meditation- Sustained concentration leads to meditation. This is an optimal time for sitting quietly.

8. Samadhi- Total Absorption- Union with the Higher Self and Universe or the state you reach as a result of meditation.

When Patanjali describes the completion of the yogic path, he speaks of what is believed all human beings aspire to: peace. Meditation is thought of then as a goal of inner peace and peace in the world. Enlightenment may be described as insight, understanding, wisdom, and knowledge – the full comprehension of a situation. Enlightenment can neither be bought nor possessed. Like meditation, it is experienced.

Vipassana Meditation

Vipassana, which means to see things as they really are, is one of India's ancient techniques of meditation. Rediscovered by Buddha, it is a way of self-transformation through self-observation and is considered a remedy for all ills. Vipassana is a non-sectarian technique that aims for clarity, happiness, and full liberation. It aims to connect the mind and body and develop a healthy mind with emphasis on the breath.

By paying close attention to the breath, and sensations connected to it, Vipassana is said to bring insight to the true nature of existence. Often it is suggested to practice this form of meditation outdoors in nature, possibly under a tree, or simply in a quiet place. Sitting with good posture energizes your meditation and strengthens the back and spine. It is important to be comfortable in your body so that your mind can find peace. Eyes are closed with natural breathing, with attention on the abdomen, as it rises and falls with your inhale and exhale. During the sitting meditation, focus remains on the breath and sensations that you experience. As your mind may drift, it is recommended that you simply label your thoughts as "thinking" and then return to the rise and fall of the breath. Similarly, if there is a loud sound as you sit, simply identify it as "hearing". This is known as a verbal label – one simple word to identify with the sensation and thought. This helps to perceive clearly the qualities of our experience, without attachment. This develops mental power and focus.

Zen or Zazen Meditation

Zazen is a type of meditation in Zen Buddhism. *Zen* is the Japanese word for meditation. *Zazen* means sitting or seated meditation. We often think of Zen as the relaxed, "chill" part of ourselves. Yet that does not describe Zen, it describes the outcome. How you feel as a result of a Zen approach to meditation or to life can be like a relief. The quiet and wise side of yourself that knows when you need to relax and letting go emerges.

Contemplation on a koan, parable or story can be a helpful way to begin Zen meditation – something to ponder, consider and contemplate outside of your current and everyday thoughts, a bigger picture to help expand your thinking. One example:

Once, a professor went to a Zen Master. He asked him to explain the meaning of Zen. The Master quietly poured a cup of tea. The cup was full but he continued to pour. The professor could not stand this any longer, so he questioned the Master impatiently, 'Why do you keep pouring when the cup is full?'

'I want to point out to you,' the Master said, 'that you are similarly attempting to understand Zen while your mind is full. First, empty your mind of preconceptions before you attempt to understand Zen'.

This is true of meditation and of daily life. Often our minds are too full to sit quietly and just be present. This is why the process is so necessary. We can learn techniques to help "empty the mind" when it is full. This alone is a difficult task to consider.

Are we really emptying our mind? Or possibly just using more of our mind, the part other than that which is already filled with thought? This too is difficult to understand. But it is attainable. By not approaching meditation with expectation we already empty the cup that is full. By not needing instant results and gratification we are on our way. Our brains are larger than we know, and we use less than we think. So, then, when we empty our mind we are really opening it, leaving room for focus and expansion.

You may ask yourself: How on earth will I empty my mind? The mind does not really empty as a cup of tea will. We need to distract and trick the mind away from conscious thoughts. This is a daunting task, the main obstacle that most of us will face. Our minds are so busy. How do we rest them?

Have you ever had the experience when you have a thought that you want to share with someone and you suddenly forget what you were going to say? Then you pause and wait and search for the thought to pop back up into your mind again? Where did the thought go? Thoughts drift when we don't want them to and won't seem to leave when we do what them too. This is the beginning of mind control and a step in the process of meditation. We can gain control, at least temporarily. This is a good reason to begin slowly and simply and notice your attention span. Keep in mind that the process of meditation is just that a process. There are steps to be taken and for good reason.

Transcendental Meditation

Transcendental Meditation (TM) is today one of the most widely used form of meditation. The Beatles popularized it in the West in 1968 when they traveled to Rishikesh, India. Their interest changed Western attitudes about meditation.

TM involves the use of mantra, which is often given by the teacher to the student for their specific, individual self. Its purpose is for stress reduction, relaxation, and self-development.

TM is taught as an effortless technique of sitting quietly two times daily for 20 minutes with the eyes closed. The mantra is often internal and therefore silent.

Words create waves of vibrations and the vibration of a mantra should correspond to the vibration of an individual. So picking a mantra that speaks to you as an individual is appropriate and a great step in the process of meditation.

Mantras are used in other types of meditation as well, such as in yoga and Kabbalah. Different types use mantras in different forms. They can be internal but are also often external, which help create a vibration in the mind and body.

Taoist Meditation

The basics of Taoist meditation are to sit still and be quiet. Different types of energy movement and exercises may be done to prepare for sitting, such as Qigong, meaning life energy cultivation. This aims to align the breath with the body for health, longevity, self-healing, self-awareness, martial arts training and meditation.

1. Stop and Observe
   Sit comfortably. Pay close attention to how thoughts arise and fade in the mind. Let them pass. This is the way to learn to not be attached to the rise and fall of emotional impulses connected to thoughts.
2. Observe and Imagine
   Visualize an image for one pointed focus.

73

3. Use the mind as an attempt to guide energy
   When the emotional mind is calm and the breath is regulated, focus attention on internal energy. Guide your energy through the body through the meridian network.

Mala Beads

Simply counting the mala beads allows for focus, mind control, distraction from thought, and a small accomplishment. It is challenging and fun, a simple tool to assist in withdrawal of the senses and distraction of the mind. It is an exercise of staying present. This prepares for a better, more still relaxation to follow, a state of meditation.

I have taught with mala beads in many kid's yoga classes, even having some students make their own. This simple counting and beading exercise requires focus that immediately quiets a classroom of children. Children too young to count to 108 can make a wrist mala of smaller amounts. You can also pick a number that is significant to you in some other way. This prepares people of all ages, even young children, to sit quietly and simply "be". It is a simple, tangible tool to be picked up at any time to signal time for focus and quiet.

Singing Bowls and Bells

Ringing a bell is a nice way to begin or end your meditation. Singing bowls each make the sound of a musical note, which can create vibration in your body and stimulate or tune into your energy. Sounding a bell at the beginning of your practice may bring you into the moment and also signal to others that you are taking time for yourself. Sounding a bell at the end may bring closure or set the tone to move on from your meditation.

Crystals and Gemstones

I have always been drawn to crystals and gemstones yet never considered applying them to my teaching. One day, sitting in quiet meditation, having voiced the obstacle aloud of teaching my students about their energy, I gained the insight to use crystals and gemstones as a means to describe qualities of our own energy in relation to the qualities of the stones.

Even though I had never made jewelry, I began making necklaces with gemstones and crystals that had healing properties and qualities in relationship to the chakras. It took no thinking. Just doing and being with the intention to teach the concept of energy and healing. As I would explain the qualities of the crystals and gemstones, people knew instinctively which one they needed. They had an object, not just an idea, to relate to. This seemed to assist them in becoming more aware of their energy, their health, balances, and imbalances. Giving them a piece of jewelry for healing increased their awareness and gave them empowerment. Suddenly, talking about energy became more tangible through this simple tool.

The relationship we have to our self and our energy, body and thoughts, is only a breath away. Noticing things in the natural world may help bring us back to our own true nature.

Visualization and imagination

In childhood, imagination is necessary and encouraged. It generally comes naturally and organically in the form of play. As we grow, we have less time for play and therefore we may not feed our imagination in the same way or at all. In our technology filled world, we may have less of a chance to be bored, which can actually inspire creativity and imagination. We can use our imagination when we begin a process of meditation, learning or re learning to use our mind to discover and rediscover our creative, playful, imaginative self. This exercise will be renewed in a grown up way for our grown up needs.

Yes, we should still find time for play and fun, song and dance. These will help get us going. But imagination for meditation will require an open mind to the new ideas you are learning here: connecting your mind and body, watching and observing your breath, imagining your energy body, seeing yourself as a whole person, thinking positive, letting go emotionally and of unwanted thoughts, setting boundaries, planning ahead and thinking intuitively. All of these will require some visualization and imagination. Even if only in your mind, you will need to be light, playful and open to new ideas and feelings. Setting the intention to meditate will be more successful if you imagine a positive outcome. Goal setting will be easier to reach if you are available to a new vision. Bring your inner child, your imaginative self to your meditation practice.

Meditation on Mandalas

Mandala is a Sanskrit word for circle. Mandalas are geometric figures representing the universe, often a square with a circle in it filled with shape and a center point. Mandalas are seen in different traditions in many forms.

Example of a Mandala

Mandalas offer a tool and visual for beginning the process of meditation. They vary in color and symbolize unity and harmony. They are designed to be visually appealing as a means to absorb the mind and inspire higher consciousness and or awareness.

A mandala may be used in meditation as a means for gaining self-knowledge. You can select a mandala that appeals to you or even draw a circle and make your own. Mandalas allow for an intention or focus. The goal is to be relaxed and find clarity. Often found in Buddhism and Hinduism, mandalas are universal in that anyone can enjoy and relax with a colorful circle symbolizing inner and universal peace.

In Tibet, mandalas are made from colored sand, and involve not only hours of creation but also destruction. In this way, they represent the transitory nature of life. The Native American mandalas symbolize the shield of good luck. In Kabbalah, the circle symbolizes the female element of creation and the square the male. The center point is nothing and everything. Mandalas are ancient, artful and fun and can be a simple form of visualization for relaxation as you begin your inner quieting journey toward a meditative state. Close your eyes and see if you can visualize it in your mind.

Meditation on Mudras

Mudras are positions of the body, particularly the hands and fingers that have an influence on the energy of your body and your mood. In yoga and Indian teachings, the physical body is made up of five elements – fire, air, water, earth, and ether or space. The balance of these elements can affect your health and immunity. When a finger representing an element is brought in touch with the thumb, the element is said to be brought into balance.

- Thumb–Fire
- Index–air
- Middle–ether
- Ring–earth
- Little–water

This is another good way to get your imagination going and distract your mind from everyday thought. As you begin to sit in meditation you can put your hands in different mudras, or positions. Sit with one finger touching the thumb and or alternating fingers, breathing as you alternate.

* * *

You may notice a particular type of meditation that you are drawn to. Try this style to begin. Learn more about it or seek a teacher with this particular style. Seeking a teacher can be key in your meditation practice and process. You may notice, like anything, the style or teacher you choose may not fit as well as you hoped. Do not be discouraged. Trial and error, effort and a positive attitude will go a long way. Have faith that you will find a fit. If you are not sure if it is the style or the teacher that is not working, get back to the basics. You can do this on your own, too. As a start, meditate for only one minute and just listen to your breathing. Contemplate and reconsider the style you chose and either try another style or find another teacher.

CHAPTER 8

THE BUILDING BLOCKS OF MEDITATION:
A BEGINNER'S TOOLBOX

*"The journey of a thousand miles begins
with a single step." -Lao Tzu*

Is it possible we all have what we need? Not everything, but enough? And if our needs are not met is it possible that they could be? Is it okay to desire more? Is desire different than dreams? Is one led by greed and the other guided by ambition? Or survival? When is enough, enough? How do we know?

Since there are many different types and techniques of meditation, we will begin by building your toolbox. With different tools and skills, you will be better able to find what makes sense for you and what you are drawn to. It is my goal to assist you in finding a technique that you will actually use, not just one to consider but actually be moved to do so. So let's begin at the beginning.

What are your current ideas of meditation? Are you an overachiever and need to master things right away? Are you competitive and always need to win? When you are beginning to learn meditation techniques, allow yourself to be a beginner. It can be humbling to see you need not conquer these skills right away. Being humble rather than frustrated is a good way to begin.

When you first begin, notice what your patience level is with yourself. Are you in a rush to grasp it? Do you need immediate results and instant gratification?

Meditation teaches us to slow down and relax. Not to rush ahead and conquer.

Pay attention

You may already be taking steps toward meditation. Since meditation is the goal and the process matters, notice how you may already be involved in the process. Begin by paying more attention to when you may actually need meditation. Notice if there are times of day when you may benefit or if there are people who you need to prepare to deal with better. Watch for the signs your body and mind give you that you need a rest or should seek help. Notice when you are helping others. Paying closer attention to how you function and what your needs actually are. Note your daily activities, how you manage your time and how you use your down time. Notice if you are easily bored or constantly stimulated.

Where might you need more balance and how might you achieve it? Thinking and thoughts are necessary and when you begin to notice them as thoughts, give them less attention so that you may make room for new thoughts. Begin to train your mind to have appropriate and useful thoughts. As you begin to address yourself as you already are, you can become more aware of your basic needs and build your foundation from the ground up. Notice your tendencies, weaknesses, and strengths. Pay attention to your symptoms. Paying attention is your teacher, as you become a good listener. Slowing down and paying attention will help you optimize the way you are already using your time. This is an ideal first step toward the benefits of meditation.

Quiet

Learning to be quiet is also an ideal and wonderful first step toward meditation. If you are already accustomed to quiet then the next step is learning to use your quiet time to your advantage. Maximizing your free time is a great way to begin a meditation practice. Do you have quiet time that comes naturally during the day? Maybe you have a moment of quiet upon waking in the morning and before falling asleep at night. Possibly you have a moment of potential quiet on your lunch break. Finding even a minute for quiet can help you to pause and slow down. While quiet is not always available, sometimes it is. Now that you are paying attention, begin to notice when quiet is available. Eventually, you may be able to achieve inner quiet even when the outer environment is not so quiet. But finding outer quiet to achieve inner quiet is a wonderful exercise with which to begin. Ideally your quiet environment is comfortable, safe, and clean. You may be sitting in a chair or on the floor, you may be lying down or even walking. Just quiet.

Not everyone enjoys silence. There are steps toward meditation that do not involve quiet. Your body and mind benefit from moving and exercising first and then sitting quiet. If quiet does not feel like the right place to start then let's look at some other beginning techniques. You can pay attention to your breath at any time. So you can still use this to bring your mind into present time.

The Breath

Once you have found some external quiet you will notice your mind may not be so quiet. Your thoughts may be lively. Your body may be uncomfortable. Your emotions may be mixed. You may have questions or doubts. You may be imaginative. You may feel emotional or even sleepy. You will need to focus here and just notice all of these things and thoughts and what comes up for you personally, not for the purpose of analysis but just to notice. As if to say, *Good to know.*

Now that you are noticing yourself, begin to pay attention to your breath.

Your breath is audible, so listen. Paying attention and listening to your breath will, at least temporarily, distract from your conscious thinking. As your mind drifts back to thought, simply refocus and begin once again to pay attention the your breath.

Your breath has two components. There is your inhalation or inspiration, the act of breathing in, and your exhalation or expiration, the act of breathing out. Notice both. It is possible one side of your breath comes more naturally while the other feels more restricted. Just notice. One side of your breath may be deeper and one more shallow. Notice. Inhale. Exhale. Simple. Try not to complicate, and continue to bring your mind back to your breath each time it wanders.

The goal here is to find a balance between your inhale and your exhale. Notice the stronger side first, but cater to your weaker side. You may be noticing that you have a balance already between your inhale and exhale. If not, then shorten the stronger side to meet up with the shorter side. The key is to find a balance in length for your inhale and your exhale. Slow your breath down. Notice.

Your breath is life. You breathe your entire life from beginning to end and may hardly notice. Or, conversely, breathing may be an issue for you and that is all you notice. If your sinuses are blocked or if you have allergies or asthma, your breath may be labored and hard to ignore.

Fresh air and good breathing revive the body and mind. A good deep breath can be stress relieving. Shallow breathing and deep breathing both have an effect on cooling and heating the body. Slowing your breath is cooling and quickening your breath is heating. Simply paying attention to your breath is a step in the process of meditation – bringing better oxygen to your body and brain, calming or stimulating the nervous system, helping to get in touch with yourself, exercising your lungs as well as your mind's ability to stay focused.

Nothingness

The funny thing is, nothingness is something. It is a subject that has been much pondered. Parmenides, one of the earliest Western philosophers considered nothing as a concept. He argued that nothing could exist by the following line of reason, that to speak of a thing, one has to speak of a thing that exists.

Doing nothing is something and is a wonderful beginning to the process of meditation. So often we do not allow ourselves to do nothing. What is the point? Might as well do something. But nothing is something, and we can learn to be disciplined with our nothing and begin to use our nothing time as our meditation time, focusing on slowing down, listening to and paying attention to the breath.

Stillness

Stillness can be inspiring, awesome and breathtaking. Picture the Grand Canyon or a still Great Lake. Moments of stillness in daily life are few so let's optimize here, too. Moving into stillness and taking pause is a wonderful beginning to meditation. Even if you cannot find quiet but can at least be still, there are benefits. Allow for the noticing of your breath and the eventual stillness of the mind. You can light a candle or sit near a window. Sit with a favorite blanket or shawl. A great way to begin stillness of the mind is to simply sit still and be quiet.

There are a few different positions that you can try out for sitting:

- Sit in a chair, preferably one that has a supportive back to help you keep good posture. One where your feet reach the floor and your can feel the ground.
- Sit crossed legged on a chair with a supportive back.
- Sit on a meditation type stool where you can place your feet on the ground underneath you, like you are kneeling.
- Sit on the floor cross-legged on a meditation pillow (zafu), towel or yoga block to boost your hips. This will make it easier on your hips and knees.
- Sit on the floor or on a pillow, towel, or block in a kneeling position.
- Sit cross-legged or kneel on the floor, towel or blanket without the use of props.

Sitting still will not only challenge your mind but also your body. It will address and strengthen your core and postural muscles, your ankles, knees, and even feet. Sitting will also create more space in your thorax for better breathing, allowing more room for your diaphragm to move and your lungs to fill with oxygen.

Notice if you are uncomfortable when you are sitting in your body. This is not a 'no pain no gain' situation. Meditation is about letting go, so be aware that you are in a position that is safe and allows you to focus on your breath. Be where you are. No forcing. Be gentle with your body. As you sit you will likely notice you fall out of good posture and begin to slouch. This is normal. Simply sit back up straight again. You are training your body and building a muscle memory when you correct and sit back up. You are also training your mind to notice and assist your body in this process. You will need strong postural muscles as you grow and age.

If you notice that you are falling asleep, maybe you are actually tired and need a nap or a rest. If this is the case, sit for one minute or even one breath at the beginning of your nap or after, or both.

Movement

It can be helpful to move your body before sitting still whenever possible. You can even simply stand up and stretch. This will often have a positive physical effect and also affect your breath. Natural cross crawl pattern movements will benefit your posture and mind–brain–body connection. You can accomplish this by taking a brisk walk, swinging your arms and deeply breathing. Also, by standing still and crossing the body hand to opposite knee a few times back and forth. Keeping the integrity of your physical body strong and balanced will provide you with a better foundation for being more physically comfortable. Physical wellness will benefit your aging process. We will need these bodies, as we get older for independent living and quality of life. Get into your body and pay attention to those needs too. Learn to exercise in a beneficial way so that then you may sit still and be focused on a healthy mind. Walking, running, hiking, biking, dancing, swimming, or whatever the movement you do, do it well and be aware of your imbalances and weaknesses to find balance and healing when getting exercise. Enjoyment is also a good factor.

Another approach to beginning a meditation practice if you are not beginning in quiet is to sing or chant. Listening to a favorite song, classical music, soulful music, drumming, bells, prayers, chanting sounds and musical scales, all stimulate your nervous system and can get you out of your head and into your heart. No need to overdo it. Moderation is good, you can kick it up a notch here and there but the basics and fundamentals will serve you well.

Movement is the way of the universe – a constant flow of planets spinning through space. We can be grounded and connected to the earth and the inner and outer worlds that are our minds and ourselves as we move in the flow of greatness, understanding and possibility.

Visualization on Color

Color is a simple way to begin the process of mindfulness and meditation. Becoming more aware of the colors around you, colors that you are naturally drawn to or colors that irritate you, colors that calm you or stimulate you. Notice the colors you choose in the clothes you wear, the colors in your home or office, the colors in the food you eat or the car you drive. You can begin a meditation with a certain color in mind to visualize, or actually surround yourself with color or artwork that you find relaxing, restoring, or revitalizing. Colors are also associated with the energy body, gemstones and birthstones and hold certain qualities.

Contemplation and Reflection

Reading or listening to a story that has meaning and provokes some contemplation may be an insightful way to begin meditation. We do not know everything, but we do know some things. Considering things we do not know and embracing ideas we do know are a form of contemplation. Contemplation focuses the mind and then begins to expand it. Consider these types of stories before you sit quietly.

Parable

A parable is a simple story used to illustrate a moral or spiritual lesson. It is a succinct, didactic story, in prose or verse, which offers one or more instructive lessons or principles. It is a type of analogy using human characters and is seen in many great religious and spiritual teachings and a tool for beginning meditation.

Koan

Based on Buddhist teachings of China, Korea, and Japan, a koan is a paradoxical question asked by Zen teachers that do not necessarily have rational answers. They use word play to assist in enlightenment. Their actual content is not as important as the state of mind that they induce. They are to be meditated upon and used to train Zen Buddhist monks to abandon ultimate dependence on reason and to force them to gain sudden intuitive enlightenment. This is said to sharpen awareness.

Students may be challenged to resolve koans in their meditation practice.

Master Hakuin Ekaku made this koan famous: "Two hands clap and there is a sound; what is the sound of one hand clapping?' The aim of a koan is to see the nonduality of a subject and object.

A few examples from the classic Zen Buddhist collection of 49 koans:

On thinking: "When you do not think good and when you do not think not-good, what is your true self?"

On speaking: "Without speaking, without silence, how can you express the truth?'

* * *

The purpose of these first steps toward meditation is creating awareness. Paying attention, listening, concentrating and focusing on your breath, finding time for movement, quiet and stillness, all are the beginning stages and will have benefits all of their own.

How and why will you actually apply and implement the knowledge you have gained? The most profound outcome of learning about your mind-body connection, your energy body, and the history and types of meditation is to actually put what you know into practice. Action is the goal of meditation even though you sit still and be quiet. A paradox. So taking baby steps and allowing for a small goal to be attainable will be a good beginning.

One breath- Become more conscious of your breath. Breath is life. Take a deep breath more often. Notice your breath more often. Balance your inhale with your exhale.

One moment- Take a moment to slow down. Slowing down and taking pause has benefits of its own.

One minute- Set a timer for one minute only. Sitting for one minute seems short and silly until you actually do it.

One mantra- Make a sound in your mind or aloud a few times in a row to distract yourself from thought and to create vibration in your mind and body.

One affirmation- Choose a positive thought to say to yourself.

One realization- Notice one important quality about yourself.

One obstacle- Notice one problem you need to resolve. Say it aloud.

One story- Read or recall a story that allows you to contemplate something about yourself or about the world.

One step- Allow yourself to progress in your practice one step at a time.

CHAPTER 9

YOUR MEDITATION PRACTICE

"Within you there is a stillness and sanctuary to which you can retreat at any time and be yourself." -Hermann Hesse

When I began formal training in meditation, we often sat in a crossed legged position on the floor for a half an hour or more. I would focus on my breath and hear the other students moving around me. Often the teachers would give no insight before or after, allow for little questioning and recommend you never move, even if discomfort arose. I was one of the only people in a room of about 100 who seemed to enjoyed this experience. I would hear a lot of complaints of discomfort, legs falling asleep (mine included), inability to "stop thinking" and general dislike of the process. Since I had already spent much time in meditation prior to these teachings, I could see my experience of going at my own pace had benefited me. I had no expectations. I did not try to "stop thinking." I allowed myself to move or look around. There were no rules. I enjoyed the practice of sitting quietly and can remember as young girl even doing a headstand before I sat. I had no judgment, no basis for comparison and no sense of what I was doing as right or wrong. Not even looking or expecting an outcome. Just being present for the sake of being present.

Sitting for long or short periods of time in meditation requires a physical, mental, and emotional discipline most people have not yet developed. This is why I give some insight into different types and suggest taking baby steps. Building postural muscles to sit for periods of time takes time and patience. Developing the skill of letting go of your feelings and thoughts also takes practice. I can recall feeling empathetic to the other students, and while I benefitted from the experience, I was sensitive to the fact that some did not.

We do not need to conquer meditation, so to speak, having a lofty goal of time and feeling unsure of the process. Nor do we need to compare ourselves to one another. What I have learned is that while we can all benefit, we may need to approach meditation very differently. Many of us will have questions. We will see better results when we are reassured. Some of us will be more natural and others my find it more difficult. Either way, it is accessible if you are true to yourself and your own needs. Begin at the beginning, wherever that may be for you. Some days you may sit longer than others and some days not at all. Some days you will feel comfortable sitting on the floor and others you may need a chair or to lie down. Some days you will have more time and other days less. Notice the emotions that come up as you begin. They may be useful to you in some way somewhere in your life.

The key is to show up in a way that you can be receptive of what is working and let go of what is not, noticing your abilities and show yourself kindness and compassion. It is not about becoming a master of meditation, but it is about becoming more of a master of yourself. Allow yourself to be unique in your individual process yet universal in your humanity.

Sample Meditation #1: One Minute

When I teach meditation, I often begin with one minute. This may seem too simple or even silly, yet it is profound. It is a reachable goal and allows for pause. Any amount of pause brings benefit. If you simply are learning to take more quiet moments, you are beginning your process in meditation. If you are currently not meditating at all, that minute is progress. If you already meditate but not consistently, then one minute is reachable more often. You could meditate one minute per hour, one minute daily, or even one minute per week. Once this has become comfortable and routine, you can begin to expand.

I time my students for one minute so there is no question. I recommend you do the same. Set the timer on your phone and have a pleasant sound on the alarm to end with. Maybe ask someone to let you know when a minute is up. Look at a clock and see for yourself. If you expand to three minutes, perhaps use a three-minute egg timer. Be practical. Be available to less is more. Once your minute is up, you can even continue sitting if you would like. Stay interested. Make reachable goals. In time, you will see the results are profound and enjoy the benefits.

One minute allows for no excuses. One minute is reachable for all. One minute allows for pause.

Sample Meditation #2: One Breath

I recommend a similar idea for your breathing. Even if you are not sitting for one minute, you can take one breath. You are breathing anyway, so one conscious breath is of benefit to your many less conscious breaths. Stress relief and mental clarity are only one breath away. Waiting in line, on the phone, on a break, approaching a person, place, or thing, improving your posture, can all be moments to benefit from a single thing, all benefitting your brain-body connection and affecting your heart rate, hormones and your "fight or flight" response.

There are many breathing techniques. Some are useful and others not so much. I recommend simply breathing more consciously in general. Slowing down your breath, breathing through your nose whenever possible. Keep it simple. Slower breathing has a calming effect on the mind and body. Nose breathing is considered better because your nose is a better filter than your mouth. So always breath in through your nose whenever possible. But you can breath out or even sigh out your exhale sometimes.

3 Sample breaths:

1. Take a deep breath, balancing inhale and exhale. You can count if you like, 3-5 each side of your breath.
2. Three small breaths in, one long breath out. Breathe in through your nose and breathe out of your nose or mouth.
3. Close one nostril and breathe in, switch to other nostril, breathe out. Breathe back in through same nostril, switch back and breath out other nostril.

Sample Meditation #3: Meditation on Your Energy Body

When you first being to meditate, especially for more than a minute, you will benefit from having a focus. Your breath is always available and is a simple focus. Yet, sometimes you may want to try to focus on something other than your breath. This is where your imagination will be useful, as you will need to visualize. You can also simply use your mind to see beyond your thoughts.

The pictures I have included in Chapter 6 may be useful. Choose the one that appeals to begin.

Example: Sefirot Meditation

- Begin sitting in good posture. Place your hands, palms face up, in your lap or on your knees. Sit strong and rooted like a tree.
- Take a breath.
- Begin to imagine your crown and the top of your head. Notice your will and your connection to the world around you. Imagine and enjoy nothingness.
- Take a breath.
- Bring the focus inward and move the energy down from the top of your head toward your forehead, knowing you have an inner understanding and wisdom.
- Take a breath.
- Continue to bring the energy down into your shoulders, heart, arms and hands, feeling loved, embracing your greatness and inner power and letting go of judgment.
- Take a breath.
- Bring your energy and focus to your center, your torso, your inner beauty and feel compassion for yourself and others.
- Take a breath.
- Continue to bring your focus down into your body to your navel and legs, storing your energy for inner endurance and feel your magnificence.
- Take a breath.

- Bring the energy down to your feet and notice your foundation and your presence.
- Take a breath.
- Sit quietly, be still and be present.

Example: Chakra Meditation

- Begin sitting in good posture. Place your hands, palms face up, on your lap or knees.
- Take a deep breath.
- Begin to imagine your first chakra at the base of your spine and the color red.
- Honor yourself and your connection to the earth.
- Take a breath.
- Move on to your second chakra below your navel and the color orange.
- Notice your inner child, your boundaries and how you move in the world.
- Take a breath.
- Move to your third chakra above your navel and the color yellow.
- Imagine your inner strength, self-confidence and success in your life.
- Take a breath.
- Now visualize your fourth chakra at your heart center and the color green.
- Have courage, be grateful and kind.
- Take a breath.
- Move the focus up to your fifth throat chakra and the color light blue.
- Imagine expressing yourself truthfully and with clarity.
- Take a breath.

- Continue up and imagine your sixth chakra or third eye at your brow and the color dark blue.
- Be open to your inner voice and knowing.
- Take a breath.
- Imagine your seventh chakra at your crown, the top of your head and the color purple.
- Feel connected.
- Take a breath.
- Now imagine above your crown and the color white and light.
- Notice how you are feeling and be in the moment.
- Take a breath.
- Begin to bring the focus back to your crown and the color purple.
- Listening to your breath.
- Now imagine dark blue at your brow.
- Relax your forehead, check in with your posture.
- Take a breath.
- Continue back down to your throat and visualize the color light blue.
- Be aware of your focus and energy moving back down through your body.
- Take a breath.
- Now see your heart giving and receiving love and the colors pink and green.
- Be relaxed.
- Take a breath.
- Moving down to your midline and the color yellow.
- Be centered.
- Take a breath.
- Now visualize below your navel and the color orange.
- Smile.
- Take a breath.

- And finally, back to the base of your spine, and the color red.
- Be grounded.
- Take a breath.
- Simply sit still and quietly.

Sample Meditation #4: Compassion

Another way to visualize and use imagery is to focus on compassion. Negative thoughts can overwhelm and sometimes take over. When you send love to yourself and others, it can replace negative thinking. Compassion is a response to the suffering of others that inspires us to help. You can give to charity and help others in ways that you can. Show respect and care for all human life and all living things. When compassion involves physically or emotionally helping others, it is appropriate and important to do so with sensitivity and sound judgment. Giving in a way that can be received boosts self-esteem, strengthens dignity and helps keep us humble. Self-compassion allows us to be kind to ourselves. It can help create positive thinking when we allow ourselves to be human and be forgiving of our mistakes. We can also give an offering to our self and others mindfully. We can simply imagine.

- Begin by sitting with good posture.
- Take a breath.
- Place your hands on your knees or lap and turn them faced open. Your heart center is connected to your hands.
- Take a breath.
- Simply imagine giving and receiving love.
- Take a breath.
- Imagine knowing when not to give and when not to receive.

- Take a breath.
- Imagine being positive and charitable with your thoughts.
- Take a breath.
- Notice your own good fortune and the good fortune of others.
- Take a breath.
- Send a blessing for those less fortunate and for your own misfortune.
- Take a breath.
- Imagine giving and receiving kindness.
- Take a breath.
- Imagine accepting who you are and the differences of others.
- Take a breath.
- Send well-wishes to yourself and others.
- Take a breath.
- Imagine inner peace and peace in the world.
- Take a breath.
- Sit quietly and be still.

Sample Meditation #5: Self-Healing

As you begin to understand and relate to your mind, brain, physical body and energy body, you may also begin to see that healing comes from within. Whether you experience health and healing through stress relief and calm or a miracle of modern medicine, you still will be experiencing healing from within. Sometimes major health issues arise needing medical attention and your body and mind will need to recover from surgery, pain, or illness. There are other times when we get by without the use of intervention. So often we take for granted our bodies ability to heal, even from a small cut or wound.

This meditation addresses your immune system, your will, and your body's ability to heal from within. Use it as a complement to your approach to your health, and as a means for personal support, relaxation, restoration, empowerment, and prevention.

- Sit or recline in good posture.
- Take a breath.
- Begin to notice your body and any areas that often demand attention.
- Take a breath.
- Begin to notice areas of your body that you never give attention to.
- Take a breath.
- As you breathe, imagine and allow your breath to carry energy through all areas of your body, head, face, hands, arms, heart and visceral organs, torso, spine, sides, legs, feet.
- Take a breath.
- Imagine your energy being balanced and flowing freely without any effort.
- Take a breath.
- Imagine what healing looks like to you.
- Take a breath.
- Begin to notice your emotions and feelings and how you view your health.
- Take a breath.
- Imagine your emotional needs are connected to your body's needs.
- Take a breath.
- Allowing feelings to rise and let them settle.
- Take a breath.
- Notice where you are disconnected and imagine being connected.
- Take a breath.

- Send yourself healing inside and out.
- Take a breath.
- Remain relaxed, quiet and still.

Sample Meditation #6: Parable

Stories that reflect on a thought and topic other than your own thoughts can be insightful as you begin your meditation practice. Sometimes a story or thought, like an affirmation, a mantra, a prayer, or even your breath, can assist you in distracting from current thought. It may even help to shed light on a particular obstacle or problem. Consider one or all of the following parables.

How we look at things, how our mind sees things, and how they really are.

Once a zookeeper said to his monkeys, "You will get three bananas in the morning and four in the afternoon." All of the monkeys were upset. "OK," he replied. "How about four bananas in the morning and three in the afternoon?" Hearing this, they are content. One should realize that sometimes change in phrasing does not represent real change.

Having Enough

Moses tells the children of Israel about God's commandments regarding manna. They are commanded to gather manna "according to what they need: one omer (ancient unit of measurement) of manna per person, per day." How can it be that people's differing needs always turn out to be a standardized portion of one omer per person per day? The commentaries explain it that the miracle that one omer per day satisfies everybody, whether they used a little or a lot. When the children of Israel actually do go out to gather manna, some gather a little and some gather a lot. Yet all receive what they need.

Obstacles

In ancient times in India, a King had a boulder placed on a roadway. Then he hid himself and watched to see if anyone would remove the huge rock. Some of the wealthiest merchants and couriers came by and simply walked around it. Many loudly blamed the king for not keeping the roads clear, but none did anything about getting the stone out of the way. Then a peasant came along carrying a load of vegetables. Upon approaching the boulder, the peasant laid down his burden and tried to move the stone to the side of the road. After much pushing and straining he finally succeeded. After the peasant picked up his load of vegetables, he noticed a purse lying in the road where the boulder had been. The purse contained gold coins and was for the person who removed the boulder from the roadway. The peasant learned what many of us never understand. Every obstacle presents an opportunity to improve our condition.

Strengths and Weaknesses

A woman has to walk down the mountainside and back up again in order to get the water she needs. She has a long pole she puts on her shoulders behind her head and places a pail on each side. Each morning she places the empty pails on the pole and begins her walk down the mountain. When she reaches the water at the bottom, she fills each pail and places them back on the pole. She then begins her long walk back up the mountain. One of the pails is old and has a crack in it. The other is new. By the time she reaches the top the old pail with the crack is always half empty. Her child finally asked, "Why do you bother to use the old, broken pail? It is always half empty and no longer useful." She replies, "I have planted flowers along the side and the broken pail with the crack waters the flowers as I walk up."

A Heavy Load

Two monks are walking along and reach a town where there is an old women struggling to cross a road where the rain had made deep puddles. The younger monk noticed the woman, said nothing, and walked by. The older monk quickly picked her up and put her on his back, transported her across the water, and put her down on the other side. The woman did not thank the older monk; she just shoved him out of the way and departed.

As they continued on their way, this was bothering the young monk. He stated that the women back there was very selfish and rude. "You picked her up and carried her on your back and she did not even thank you!" The older monk replied, "I set that women down hours ago. Why are *you* still carrying her?"

Troubles Tree

There was a carpenter who worked hard building houses all day. He had a difficult day: a flat tire made him lose an hour of work, his electric saw broke, and he could not start his old truck to go home. He needed to ask the man he was working with for a ride. During the ride, he sat in silence. On arriving, he invited the man in to meet his family. As they walked to the door, he paused briefly at a tree, touching the branches with his hands. When opening the door, he went through an amazing transformation. He smiled and hugged and kissed his wife and two small children.

After, he walked the man out to his car. When they passed the tree the man asked about why the man touched the tree earlier when they arrived and before entering his house. The man replied: "Oh, that is my "troubles tree". I know I cannot help having troubles on the job, but I can help to not bring them home to my family. So, every night when I come home I hang them on the tree. Then, in the morning I pick them up again. But the thing is that when I come out in the morning, there are not nearly as many troubles as I remember hanging up the night before."

Sample Meditation #7: Mandala

Mandalas are used to facilitate meditation. The geometric patterns represent the cosmos metaphysically or symbolically. You can simply look at or visualize one and allow it to have an effect on your mind. They can have a calming and balancing influence and can help to quiet a restless mind. After viewing a mandala, sit quiet and imagine it in your mind.

Sample Meditation #8: Mudra

Hand positions and gestures are used universally for self-expression. We use our hands when we talk. Sign language is a form of speech. We use the OK sign, the peace sign and other gestures with our fingers. These are a form of communication with no words being necessary. Hand positions in meditation also evoke a type of communication, but with yourself. Speaking silently to yourself with an intention to heal, balance, restore and connect with higher aspects of yourself and or the universe.

Hand positions can be relaxing and a focal point for the mind. When you sit in meditation, choose a hand position that feels comfortable. Some examples for your meditation are:

- Sit or stand in a comfortable position with good posture.
- Place hands in front of you and in lap if sitting.
- Place one palm in the other facing up in a receiving position.
- Breathe.
- Imaging receiving love through your hands into your heart.

Another example is to, again, sit or stand in a comfortable position with good posture.

- Place your hands in front of you on your lap or knees if sitting cross-legged.
- Palms face up.
- Touch your finger with your thumb (you can even alternate all fingers).
- Breathe.
- Relax.
- Receive energy through your hands and allow it to flow through your body with your breath.
- This is a good time to smile, lighten up and simply be.

Sample Meditation #9: Mantra

When used externally and said aloud, mantras produce a sound, which has an effect on your body and mind. You can also say them silently in your mind. Choose a mantra that appeals to you. I have given examples below or you can use the sounds in Chapter 6 in relation to the chakras. You can take in a deep breath and recite the mantra on your exhale. Choose to make the sound once or repeat the sound a number of times. Listen to the sound of your breath as you inhale and continue listening to the sound of the mantra as you exhale.

Examples of Mantras:

- Om/Aum is a mystical sound described as a primordial vibration of the earth.
- Do Re Me Fa So La Ti can be said individually or as a whole.
- Shalom
- Hum
- Ahh
- Mmm
- Ha

After the reciting or chanting of a mantra, simply sit quietly.

* * *

Getting to Mindfulness

Mindfulness is an alert awareness of what is going on. Exercises in mindfulness help concentration, while development of concentration helps develop mindfulness.

Both help memory. Memory is defined as a process in which information is encoded, stored and retrieved. So as you learn life's many lessons and experience many obstacles, you can create new and improved memories in your body and mind and remain more present more often. Observe the past as a means for healing, always returning to the present moment to get grounded.

Being mindful helps in the meditation process since you are learning to pay more attention to being in the moment. Becoming more aware and focused on what you are actually doing can affect the outcome. By being more mindful you are naturally slowing down and tapping into the more focused part of your brain. Being mindful of your breathing could mean taking a deep breath a few times a day – not because you are stressed or did not even mean to, but just for the sake of it. Take a deep breath for prevention of future stress. Preparing for what life brings even in your mind is a healing exercise – seeing situations for what they really are and approaching them appropriately, having clarity and taking pause.

Being mindful is really a way of living. Being aware of what's going on is actually a skill. Indeed, it is also a step in the process toward meditation. Mindfulness is a choice and a simple state of mind to agree to hold integrity in our lives. Being mindful means:

- Taking pause, having clarity and conscious thought
- Being more present and in the moment
- Paying attention to our thinking
- Finding emotional balance, courage, kindness, inner calm, forgiveness, acceptance and gratitude
- Listening to our breath and our intuition, our inner knowing
- Threading our mind-body connectedness to form the whole person you are
- Using freedom well, as well as free time

The more mindful we are, the more we see there is plenty of time to meditate and many ways to do so. The reasons to do so are simple and profound.

Mindfulness is reachable and only a breath away.

There is a paradox here. *Are we actually over thinking our meditation practice?*

Are we thinking too much by trying not to think? Are we falling asleep or being overwhelmed by trying to stop the mind from thinking? Are we overdoing it and eventually avoiding it all together? Are we complicating the idea of sitting still and being quiet? Maybe we are trying too hard to attain something rather than simply being present. Slowing down, connecting with our self, is it really something we need to master?

Conversely, are we swinging and missing when we give up and imagine meditation as something unattainable? After all, it is age old and many have tried and even devoted their entire lives to meditation. So then who do we think we are by even approaching meditation or the process, as if it is attainable, if we are only sitting for a silly minute? Why bother? Especially, if it is a bother.

I have seen numerous personal results in myself and in my students. The benefits are endless and attainable. What we need, even once in a while, is to simply be quiet. When that time is up, try it again sometime.

Although it is possible that you see results every time you meditate, give yourself up to eight weeks to see results. When studies on meditation and the brain have been done in the form of MRI, eight-week programs are sometimes given. Other than the immediate pause a deep breath can bring, and the benefit a little quiet and positive thinking can do, be patient and give yourself some time to try a couple of techniques. You can even alternate techniques. Check in from day to day or even week to week and do what works at the time. But do something. A little goes a long way and do not be discouraged. In fact, be encouraged.

After sitting in meditation, you may begin to notice you are no longer tied to your thoughts all the time. You may also notice you are making less excuses for needing the quiet. You may begin with a technique or a specific amount of time but then notice you "forgot" about the time and maybe even stopped noticing your thoughts or that you are sitting at all. You may think you dozed off or zoned out, but possibly you may have let go to an even higher state of mind than you thought possible. You allowed yourself to be present and let go of even technique and time. This is a sign that you are not only learning to focus your thoughts and mind, but are actually beginning to expand.

Being more present and having more moments of pause is something everyone can implement, though each of us will have a different experience and story to tell. The result of self-realization, experiencing nothingness, and becoming more intuitive and interconnected may vary. What will it be for you?

Your state of mind and cognitive process is individual and the evolution of your meditation will be as well. You may reach a higher or different state of mind when in quiet stillness, thinking, and then letting thoughts pass, breathing, and then thinking again. Suddenly, without effort or even knowing, there is an absence of conscious thoughts and a lost sense of time – and then suddenly a return to present time thinking and noticing senses again. This experience feels like a relief, a gift and a type of surrender. Reaching different states of mind, or even a blissful state, being oblivious to everything else, is attainable in meditation. Happiness is also a state of mind reachable but remember that happiness comes from within. Emotions come and go. Having meaning and purpose in life is long lasting. Pay attention to the process you take. Small steps and goals and taking credit for each step big or small can go a long way. Letting go of frustration and being okay with little or no results initially will allow for results unseen before to show, not being attached to an outcome but setting an intention. If letting go is not attainable right away then try to *Let it Be.*

Some will reach higher states of mind more easily and readily. Others will need more time. Some will do this naturally and on their own. Others will benefit more with feedback, guidance, and a teacher. Either way, benefits are there for everyone.

Be aware that as you begin and focus either on your spirit, mind, emotions, or body, that the goal is to become integrated – seeing yourself as a whole by noticing your parts and different aspects of yourself. As you begin to notice why and when you need meditation, you will become more tuned in to the parts of you that need healing or attention. Once you notice, you can pull yourself together, so to speak. Embracing the wisdom of wholeness within yourself, and bringing that wisdom with you as you express yourself in the world.

Positive thinking requires positive thoughts. Finding purpose and meaning in life is a reachable goal and the journey matters. Our goals will need a balance with our approach. Be realistic and reasonable. Be available to baby steps or even profound change. Keep it simple. You decrease stress and improve well-being by checking in with your needs, your breath and taking good care of yourself. By being more present, more mindful and interconnected, you can create more balance and awareness. By simply taking pause and finding time for a little quiet, you are in the process of and learning how to meditate and why.

AFTERWORD

I'm the last guy you would think of when the subject of meditation arises. Aggressive. Type A. Workaholic. But after reading Mara's book, I have found a way to meditate in a way that works for me. This book taught me that meditation is not a rigorous routine of do's and don'ts, but rather an approach to handle the unceasing challenges of life. Once you understand meditation, you can apply it as you see fit.

In reading this book, I realized that although I did not know much about meditation, I was doing some form of it already in the way I led my life. Now I see, with small alterations, that I can develop my methods and get even more benefit from it. Some examples of "my meditation" are getting up very early and being at work at 5am, then spending the first 15 minutes clearing my mind by sitting quietly and then visualizing the day. Another way is spending time with my pets. They know how to stay in the moment, and they help me do the same. I've also always enjoyed running, and the "zone" I lock into is a form of meditation. Hearing my breath is mind clearing.

Finally, until reading this book, I never fully realized the relationship between intuition and meditation. In all of my business roles, I've surely counted on facts, but intuition or "gut feelings" also played an important role. This book gives insights into how to develop, use, and trust your intuition to help improve your decision-making in life. There are so many aspects of meditation that can enrich your life. Mara does a great job of not constraining with rules but rather expanding with flexibility. I'm confident that you will benefit from this read just as I did. Yet there is more – not only will you learn the why and how's of meditation, you will also gain a concise history and broader view of how and where the practice developed. *How to Meditate and Why* offers a great way to learn about meditation and apply it to your life so you can get the most out of it.

-Larry Zimmerman, Retired Vice Chairman and CFO, Xerox (and proud father)

REFERENCES AND FURTHER READING

Chatterji, J.C. *The Wisdom of the Vedas*. Wheaton, Illinois: Theosophical Publishing House, 1992.

Choquette, Sonia. *True Balance*. New York: Harmony Publishing Co., 2010.

Hesse, Hermann. *Siddhartha*. New York: Directions Publishing Co., 1951.

Iyengar, B.K.S. *The Tree of Yoga*. Boston: Shambhala Publications, Inc., 1988.

Jung, C.G. *The Archetypes and the Collective Unconscious*. New York: Princeton University Press, 1969.

Kaplan, Aryeh. *Meditation and Kabbalah*. San Francisco: Weiser Books, 1982.

Krishnamurti, Jiddu. *Think on These Things*. New York: Harper and Row, 1964.

Matt, Daniel C. Translation of *The Zohar, Pritzker Edition*. Stanford, California: Stanford University Press, 2004.

Roach, Geshe Michael and McNally, Lama Christie. *The Diamond Cutter*. New York: Harmony Publishing Co., 2009.

Satchidananda, Sri Swami. *The Yoga Sutras of Patanjali*. Buckingham, Virginia: Integral Yoga Publications, 2012.

Shaku, Soyen. Translation Senzaki, Nyogen. *The Gateless Gate: 49 Zen Koans*. Kindle Edition, 1934.

Tzu, Lao. Translation Muller, Charles, *Tao Te Ching*. New York: Barnes and Noble, 2005.

Walker, Brian Browne. *The I Ching or Book of Changes: A Guide to Life's Turning Points*. New York: St. Martin's Press, 1992.

Wiesel, Elie. *Messengers of God*. New York: Random House, 1976.

Yogananda, Paramhansa. *Autobiography of a Yogi*. New York: Crystal Clarity, 1946.